CONTENTS

KV-676-661

So you know ...

This book is all about using Publisher, which is what we call a desktop publishing program, or DTP for short. This is a program that allows you to easily create documents that include both text and images, such as in a magazine or newspaper.

You will first learn some of the skills needed to use Publisher and then you will be asked to make decisions about the kinds of documents and images needed for a particular audience and purpose. This will allow you to show your capability in using ICT and achieve higher National Curriculum levels.

The skills you will learn are:

Task 1: How to create a document and manipulate images.
Task 2: How to create a style.
Task 3: How to create a document that can be email merged.

You will then be able to use all of the skills you have learnt and the files you have created to carry out the **final project**.

You are eventually going to create an advert and ticket that can be emailed for a band advertising its latest concert. When you have the learned the skills to create everything you'll need, it will be up to you to decide how to use your skills to create the look and feel of your advert and ticket.

This screenshot is an example of the features you will be using in Publisher and the type of document you can create:

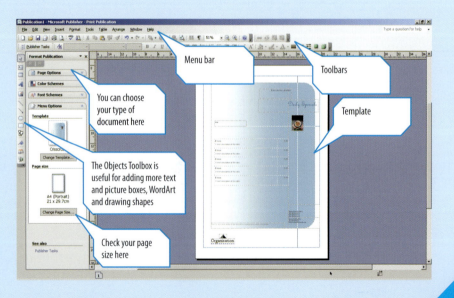

Figure Intro.1

basic PROJECTS

Publisher
2007

> John Giles

www.payne-gallway.co.uk

✓ Free online support
✓ Useful weblinks
✓ 24 hour online ordering

01865 888070

PAYNE-GALLWAY

Payne-Gallway is an imprint of Pearson Education Limited, a company incorporated in England and Wales, having its registered office at Edinburgh Gate, Harlow, Essex, CM20 2JE. Registered company number: 872828

www.payne-gallway.co.uk

Text © John Giles 2008

First published 2008

12 11 10 09 08
10 9 8 7 6 5 4 3 2 1

British Library Cataloguing in Publication Data
A catalogue record for this book is available from the British Library.

ISBN 978 1 905292 53 8

Copyright notice
All rights reserved. No part of this publication may be reproduced in any form or by any means (including photocopying or storing it in any medium by electronic means and whether or not transiently or incidentally to some other use of this publication) without the written permission of the copyright owner, except in accordance with the provisions of the Copyright, Designs and Patents Act 1988 or under the terms of a licence issued by the Copyright Licensing Agency, Saffron House, 6–10 Kirby Street, London EC1N 8TS (www.cla.co.uk). Applications for the copyright owner's written permission should be addressed to the publisher.

Designed by Wooden Ark Studios
Edited and typeset by Sparks – www.sparkspublishing.com
Cover design by Wooden Ark Studios
Printed in China CTPS

Acknowledgements
Every effort has been made to contact copyright holders of material reproduced in this book. Any omissions will be rectified in subsequent printings if notice is given to the publishers.

Original Slurp can design by Frances Sharp.

Websites
The websites used in this book were correct and up-to-date at the time of publication. It is essential for tutors to preview each website before using it in class so as to ensure that the URL is still accurate, relevant and appropriate. We suggest that tutors bookmark useful websites and consider enabling students to access them through the school/college intranet.

Ordering Information
Payne-Gallway, FREEPOST (OF1771),
PO Box 381, Oxford OX2 8BR
Tel: 01865 888070
Fax: 01865 314029
Email: orders@payne-gallway.co.uk

This book also helps you to develop your Functional Skills in ICT. This is all about you being able to use your software skills in the way that best suits the activity that you have been given – in other words *why* you are doing something in the way that you have chosen. For example, you always need to be thinking about the purpose of what you are doing – what has it got to do with the activity, what kind of impact do you want to achieve, who is going to see or use what you're working on, i.e. who is your audience, and what is the background of the situation – for example, do you need to produce a formal or informal document? By considering all of these things you should be able to produce the right kind of documents that are 'fit for purpose', i.e. they do the job they need to do. A lot to take in at once I know, but have a look at the Functional Skills tabs as you work through the book and they'll show you what all this means in practice… so that you can use them to help you with your project.

Before we start with Task 1, though, the next few pages show you some of the most important skills that you'll need throughout your whole project; how to start the program, create new files and save your work. Remember you can return to these pages to remind yourself of these skills if you forget later on in the project. Although this shows the 2007 version of Publisher, the instructions will work equally well with previous versions, such as 2003.

FIRING IT UP!

There are two ways to start Publisher.

Either

 Double click its icon on the desktop.

Figure Intro.2

Or

 Open Publisher from the **Start** menu:

Figure Intro.3

Creating a new file

Click on Start and then follow the numbers. (This screen will not look exactly like yours.) When Publisher loads, the first screen that you see is the Getting Started screen – see Figure Intro.4.

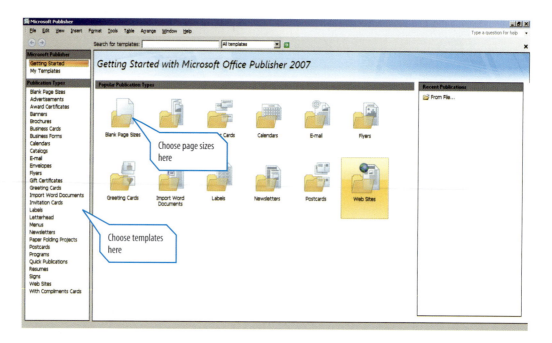

Figure Intro.4

You can use this screen to:

❱ choose the page size

❱ choose one of the already made templates.

Page size and paper size

Your printer will have paper of a certain paper size already loaded into it. This is likely to be A4 size and probably can't be changed easily.

Publisher allows you to choose page sizes for your work displayed on the screen. For instance, you can choose a smaller page size for a greetings card. If you choose a larger page size than the size of the paper in your printer, then your printer may use several sheets of paper to print your work. So choosing a page size of A3 would mean that your printer would use two sheets to print your publication.

Templates

Templates are a way of reducing the amount of work that we have to do.

A template is an already part-designed publication; have a look at 'Advertisements' and 'Award Certificates' to get some idea of the range of templates already in Publisher. You can probably think of some immediate uses for one or two of these templates. If there isn't a template for the task that you are carrying out, you can design a new template and then store it here so that you can use it time and time again. That can save a lot of work.

Figure Intro.5

You can even go online and find more templates on the Microsoft site.

Styles

Styles is another handy feature of Publisher that helps to speed up your work. Look at the right-hand pane of the window on your screen. Make sure you have the Award Certificates templates loaded and then:

   Click on one of the templates.

Notice that a larger view of the template appears in the right-hand pane, as shown in Figure Intro.6. Click on the drop-down **Color Scheme** option in the **Customize** box.

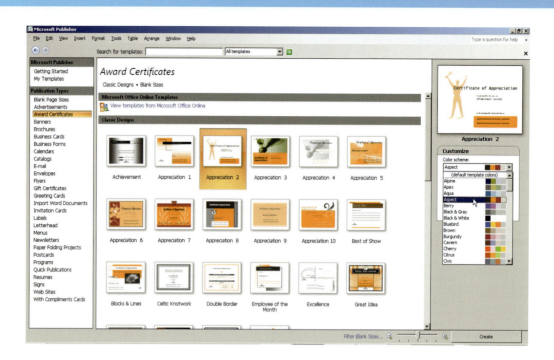

Figure Intro.6

Notice that the colour style changes when you click another group of colours.

 Try changing the font styles.

 Turn all of the styles settings back to Default.

Sometimes, though, you don't want a Template and just a Blank Page is useful. The next screenshot shows some of the different sizes available.

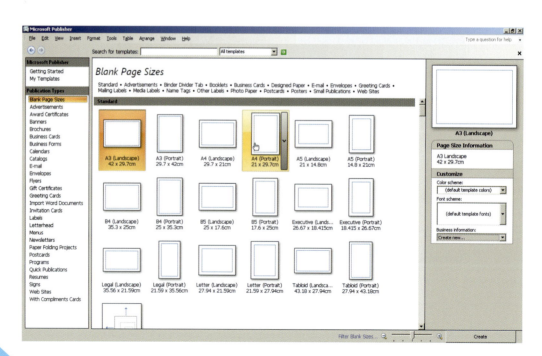

Figure Intro.7

4   Have a look at the Blank Page Sizes and think for what purpose you could use some of them.

SAVING A FILE

You can save the document as it is in the normal way by finding or making a folder:

 1   Click on **File** on the menu bar and then select **Save As**.

2   In the Save As dialogue box, make the settings as in Figure Intro.8.

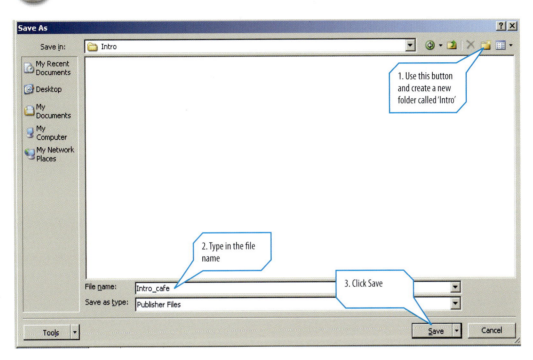

Figure Intro.8

Saving as a template

This is useful where you think you might need to use the layout again for the start of another document.

 1   Click on File on the menu bar and select Save As.

 2   Make the changes as in Figures Intro.9 and Intro.10.

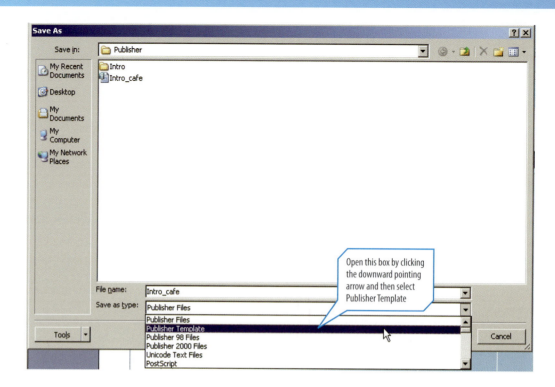

Figure Intro.9

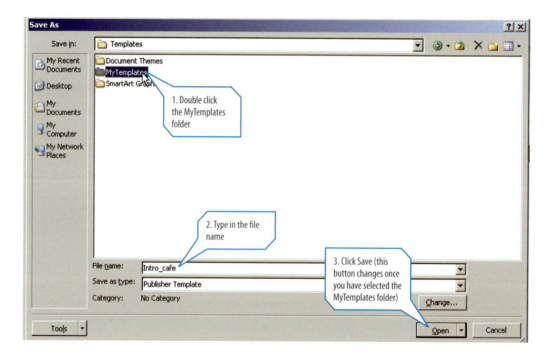

Figure Intro.10

 Now check that all is well by clicking **File** on the menu bar and selecting **New**.

Click My Templates in the Microsoft Publisher pane on the left-hand side of the screen.

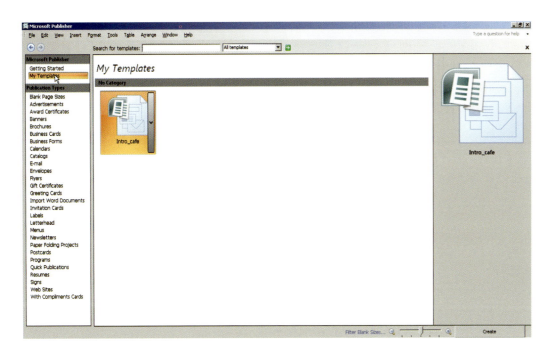

Figure Intro.11

DESIGNING AN ADVERT

TASK BRIEF

You work for Design Studio and you have just received this email ...

BACKGROUND

Slurp is a new, healthy, sugar-free canned drink aimed at 9–14-year-olds and is produced by Big Drinks Ltd.

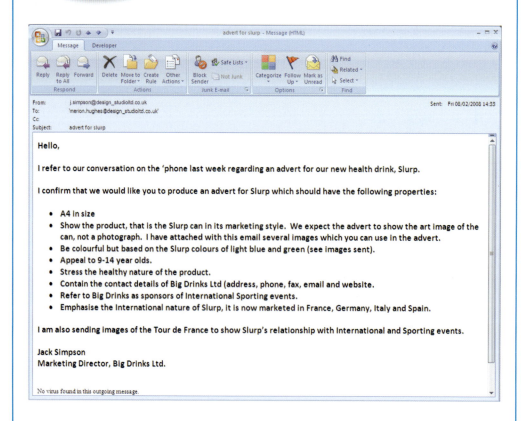

advert for slurp - Message (HTML)

Message	Developer	

Reply | Reply to All | Forward | Delete | Move to Folder | Create Rule | Other Actions | Block Sender | Safe Lists | Not Junk | Categorize | Follow Up | Mark as Unread | Find | Related | Select

Respond | Actions | Junk E-mail | Options | Find

From: j.simpson@design_studioltd.co.uk   Sent: Fri 08/02/2008 14:33
To: 'merion.hughes@design_studioltd.co.uk'
Cc:
Subject: advert for slurp

Hello,

I refer to our conversation on the 'phone last week regarding an advert for our new health drink, Slurp.

I confirm that we would like you to produce an advert for Slurp which should have the following properties:

- A4 in size
- Show the product, that is the Slurp can in its marketing style. We expect the advert to show the art image of the can, not a photograph. I have attached with this email several images which you can use in the advert.
- Be colourful but based on the Slurp colours of light blue and green (see images sent).
- Appeal to 9-14 year olds.
- Stress the healthy nature of the product.
- Contain the contact details of Big Drinks Ltd (address, phone, fax, email and website.
- Refer to Big Drinks as sponsors of International Sporting events.
- Emphasise the International nature of Slurp, it is now marketed in France, Germany, Italy and Spain.

I am also sending images of the Tour de France to show Slurp's relationship with International and Sporting events.

Jack Simpson
Marketing Director, Big Drinks Ltd.

No virus found in this outgoing message.

Figure 1.1

SOFTWARE SKILLS

You will learn how to:

❯ Select and modify a template for a specific purpose

❯ Plan and produce a layout for a document

❯ Add and change images

❯ Make and save files and templates

❯ Save resources in the Content Library

FUNCTIONAL SKILLS

As you work through this task the Functional Skills tabs will explain to you why the task tackles the brief in the way shown here and explain why you would choose to:

❯ Plan and create a document and layout

❯ Use a template

❯ Match font styles and colour with the audience

❯ Select images

❯ Organise your files and folders

❯ Choose particular software

CAPABILITY

In this task you are learning the skills that will help you to be able to make the appropriate decisions according to the audience and purpose on future projects.

VOCABULARY

You should understand the meaning of these words that may be new to you:

❯ Template

❯ Style

❯ Navigate

❯ Content Library

Always use the spellings we use in Britain in your writing even if you see the US spellings in the software, e.g. use 'colour' and not the US equivalent, 'color'.

RESOURCES

There are three files for this task:

SlurpCan_1.jpg

TourDeFrance_1.jpg

You can download these files from www.payne-gallway.co.uk

⊕ TARGET POINT

Turn the page to see your Target Points for this task.

Level 3	Level 4	Level 5	Level 6
You have saved your work	You have saved your work as a template		
You have used a new template	You have used the Style controls to modify an existing template, including changes to show that you understand layering	You have used the Style controls to change an existing template and used it to make the style of your documents consistent	You have created your own style sheet and used it to make the style of your documents consistent
	You have combined different forms of information into your document and styled it appropriately for your audience		
		You have made your document suitable for an unfamiliar audience	
	You have used the criteria and met most of the requirements of the brief	You have used the criteria and met all of the requirements of the brief and produced a template appropriate for the target audience	

TARGET POINT

Have a look at the following statements before you start your task so that you know what you are aiming for.

Although you will not make your own decisions on the design of the template in Task 1, you can use what you learn here to help with other work that will be awarded a particular level.

FUNCTIONAL SKILLS

Organising your files and folder structure – you should keep your folders organised so that you can keep your work for each project stored separately and you should store your files using suitable names so that you can find an individual file easily

FUNCTIONAL SKILLS

Choosing the best software to meet your needs means that your task will be completed in the most efficient and effective way – in this example we have chosen Publisher because it is the best software package available to us for working on documents that include several images

OK. Let's get started.

Before you start any project, you should organise your folders where you are going to save the work.

 Create a new folder called **Publisher**.

 In the Publisher folder, create another folder called **Task1** – this is where you will save the files you will be creating.

Choosing software for the task

You could use either a word processor or a desktop publishing (DTP) application like Publisher for this job. In this case it would be better to use DTP, because you will need the option of moving around blocks of text (such as information on the drink) and images (such as the picture of the Slurp can).

Template

It would save a lot of time if we could find a template that we could use as a layout for the advert. There are a number of templates that would be suitable in the Flyers group.

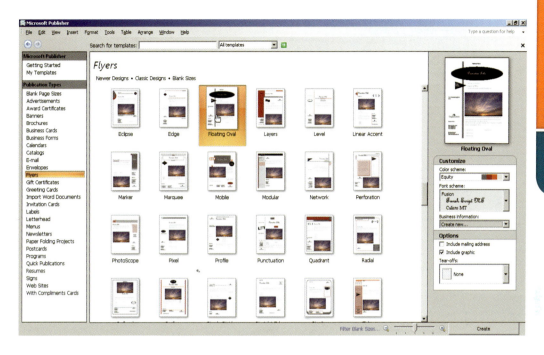

FUNCTIONAL SKILLS

Choosing the right template or document - layout is important because it helps with getting the message to the reader – in this case we need the information to be clear and immediately obvious as it's an advert to promote a product so a flyer template is appropriate

SOFTWARE SKILLS

Using a template

Figure 1.2

Have another look at the email and think of the main items that will be needed for the advert; this will help you to choose the best template. The main requirements are:

- A4 size.

- A place for the title.

- A picture of the Slurp can.

- A sporting picture.

- A text box for the contact details.

- A text box to emphasise the healthy nature of Slurp.

- A text box to emphasise the sporting connection with Slurp.

Other requirements such as colour and making the advert appeal to 9–14-year-olds can be done later once we have settled on a layout.

Have a look at the template 'Floating Oval'.

Figure 1.3

That just leaves the need for a space for the picture of the Tour de France, which needs to appear in the advert. Using the picture as the background would solve this.

DESIGNING AN ADVERT

 We are going to load the template and then apply the changes to style.

Double click the **Floating Oval** template.

 Click **Flyer Options** in the Tasks pane on the left-hand side of the screen.

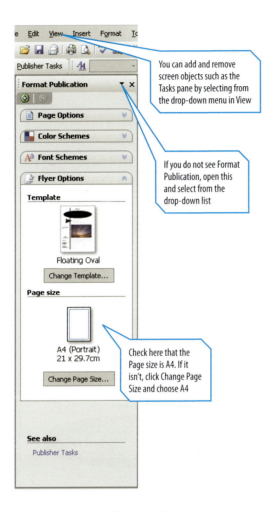

Figure 1.4

Make sure that the **Page Size** is set to A4 and, if not, follow the instructions in Figure 1.4.

You need to modify the **Color Scheme**: none of the preformed colour schemes are going to be a match to the colours used on the Slurp can, so we will need to make our own colour scheme.

First of all, we need a copy of the image of the Slurp can so that we can match the colours of the new Color Scheme.

FUNCTIONAL SKILLS

The use of colour is important to consider for a document that is designed to attract attention but here we are using the colours of the product the advert is promoting to keep the colours used consistent and so that people will associate the colours with the product

 Click **Insert** on the menu bar and then select **Picture** from the shortcut menu and **From File** on the sub-menu.

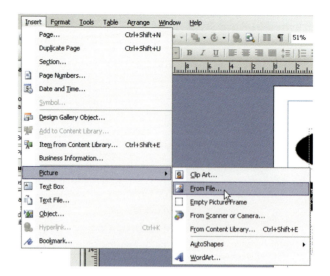

Figure 1.5

Now navigate to the folder that contains the images of Slurp.

Open the **SlurpCan_1** file.

You will see the image on the template.

Figure 1.6

Don't try to insert the image into your template; all we are doing at this stage is to set up the colour scheme to be used in the advert, not the content of the advert (which will be dealt with later).

Since we are likely to use this image several times, it would be useful to have the image stored in a handy place. Fortunately, Publisher has this already for you!

 Click the drop-down box in the Tasks pane and select **Content Library**.

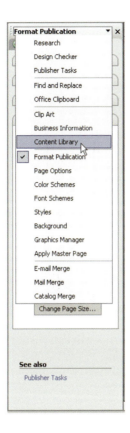

Figure 1.7

 Make sure that the picture of the Slurp can is highlighted. If it doesn't show the handles as in Figure 1.8, click on it.

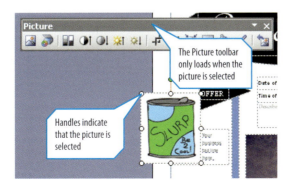

Figure 1.8

SOFTWARE SKILLS
Adding images to the Content Library

Click **Add selected items to Content Library**.

The Add Item to Content Library dialogue box loads.

Figure1.9

It is sensible to add the picture to the **Business** category, as is shown in Figure 1.9.

 Click **OK**.

The image is added to the Content Library and appears in the library as a thumbnail.

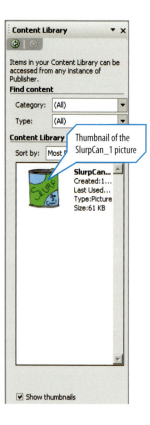

Figure 1.10

You can now easily re-use the image whenever you need to.

Matching the new colour scheme to the can

 10 Click on the drop-down box in the Tasks pane and this time select **Color Schemes**.

Figure 1.11

SOFTWARE SKILLS
Applying colour schemes

 11 Towards the bottom of the Apply Color Schemes window you will see **Create new color scheme**. Click it!

It's obvious that the **Main** part of the current scheme does not match the colours used in the can image – it's black!

 12 Open the **New** drop-down box.

 13 None of the colours offered seems close to the blue used on the can, so click the **More Colors** option at the bottom.

Figure 1.12

The **Colors** palette opens.

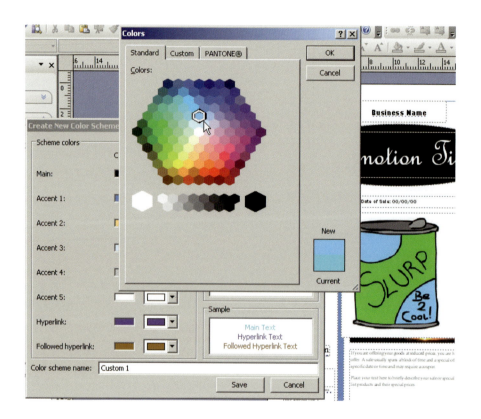

Figure 1.13

Position the colour palette close to the image of the Slurp can so that you are able to compare the colour selected with that of the can.

Try out a few colours. When you think you have a good match, click **OK**.

Notice that the thumbnail in the Create New Color Scheme dialogue box has been updated, so you can see the effect on the template – that's pretty useful!

The next job is to change the Accent 1 colour to the green used on the Slurp can. You can do this as you did for the Main colour.

 When you have finished changing the colours of the Color Scheme (not all of the colours are used so don't bother with changing them all), type in a suitable Color Scheme name such as SlurpCan_AdvertScheme.

 Click **Save**.

 Look at the Color Schemes box. You will see that the new scheme has been incorporated into the existing schemes.

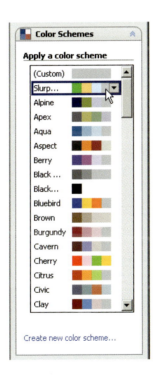

Figure 1.14

Selecting a suitable Font Scheme

FUNCTIONAL SKILLS

Choosing an appropriate font for your audience and purpose is very important – as our flyer is to attract 9-14 year olds we are going to use a font style that looks fun and quirky but is still clear to read. The font also matches the style used on the can so we can be consistent and the style of writing becomes recognised with the product

SOFTWARE SKILLS

Changing a font style

18 Open the **Font Schemes** box.

Figure 1.15

The casual style of the letters used on the can might be difficult to match, but have a look to see if there are Font Schemes that you think would do.

19 Unfortunately it seems unlikely that any of the current Font Schemes will be useful, so click on **Create New Font Scheme**.

Select a new font for the **Heading** and **Body**. In this example Kristen ITC and Bauhaus 93 have been used, but you might prefer to use other fonts. Body means the continuous writing used in the advert: in our case this will be used for the contact details and information about the healthy nature of Slurp.

Figure 1.16

20 Type in a name for the Font Scheme.

 21 Click **Save**.

The new Font Scheme appears as an addition in the Font Schemes box.

Figure 1.17

Well, that's our font sorted out, so let's tackle the layout of the advert.

Improving the layout

FUNCTIONAL SKILLS

Selecting suitable images – we have to consider these things when selecting images:

- *our clients requirements*
- *the audience*
- *the file size (this is important if you want to use the image electronically because large files take a long time to open)*
- *the amount of money we have to spend on the images (the budget)*
- *copyright*

Here, the client has supplied several images but we chose this one because it matches the company's links with international sporting events and is highly colourful (appealing to 9–14 year olds). The image has been supplied to us so we don't need to worry about budget or copyright as the client has given us permission to use their image. If you don't own the image, you'll need to contact the owner (copyright holder) for permission to use it

22 The layout of the template could do with improving because there are too many text boxes for our needs.

Delete all of the text boxes except for those which are shown in Figure 1.18.

Figure 1.18

Notice that the original picture has been deleted and the Slurp can image is now used instead.

The only other item that we need to add to the template is the sporting image, which is a requirement in the Big Drinks email.

23 Add the image TourDeFrance_1 to the Content Library.

24 Place the TourDeFrance_1 picture over the advert page.

25 Make sure that the image fits to the blue line showing the margins of the page.

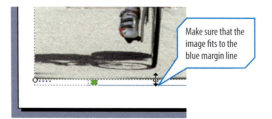

Make sure that the image fits to the blue margin line

Figure 1.19

The picture will obscure all of the rest of the template because it is 'in front' of all of the other objects on the template. You need to send the picture to the back so that the title, etc., becomes visible again.

 26 Make sure that the picture is highlighted.

 27 Click on the **Arrange** icon on the menu bar and select **Order** from the shortcut menu and then **Send to Back** from the sub-menu.

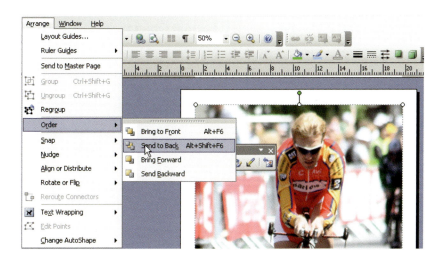

Figure 1.20

This results in the Slurp can re-appearing but with an unattractive white border.

Removing the image's white border

 28 Make sure that the Slurp can picture is highlighted.

 29 Click the **Set Transparency Color** button on the **Picture** toolbar.

Figure 1.21

This tool allows you to make any selected colour transparent, so now it's just a case of selecting the white border.

 30 Click anywhere on the white border.

Magic – the border has gone! Now have a look at the other features on the advert and let's see how we can improve them.

Improving the shapes

 31 Resize and move the shape.

The triangle and the oval shape around the title are blocking too much of the picture and would be better if we could see through them. Let's see how we do this.

 32 Click on the triangle so that it is highlighted.

 33 Right click on the triangle and select **Format Object** from the shortcut menu.

The Format Object dialogue box loads.

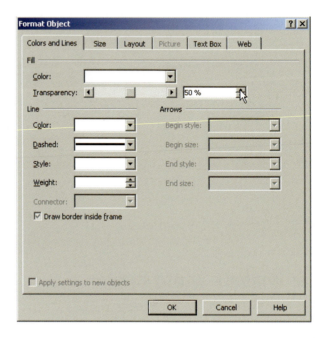

Figure 1.22

 34 Swap to the **Colors and Lines** tab and set the Transparency to about 50%.

 35 Click **OK** and view the effect.

 36 Repeat on the title oval shape.

The colour is not as bright, but the background image is visible so it achieves what we need.

The texts for the name of the company, its address and the 'health' information have not been added yet, but we should save the template now that the basics of the layout are established.

 37 Save your advert as **SlurpAdvert_Template1** in your **Task 1** folder.

Preview

 It's useful to have a look at the advert without the interference of the lines around text boxes and picture frames.

Click on the **Print Preview** button  on the Standard toolbar.

Figure 1.23

ALL DONE

Task 1 is now complete.

Now we're going to send this to Big Drinks and make sure that they're happy with the design before we add any more text like their contact details and their sponsorship, which they requested us to add in their brief.

FUNCTIONAL SKILLS

When working on documents for a client, you should always try and get their feedback after each stage of the design to make sure that you are creating what they want. You should then discuss any changes that they suggest and adapt your document as necessary. Remember, it's not about what you like – it's about what meets the needs of your client and their audience

CHECKPOINT

Check that you know how to:

➤ Select a page size.

➤ Select a template.

➤ Change the colour style of a template.

➤ Change the font style of a template.

➤ Save a template.

➤ Save a useful image in the Content Library.

➤ Navigate to find a file.

➤ Place a picture in a Publisher document.

➤ Resize a text box and picture frame.

➤ Delete a text box and picture frame.

➤ Format an image: fill colour, transparency.

➤ Use the Order control to move images to the back and forwards to alter their visibility in the finished document.

ASSESSMENT POINT

Now let's assess the work. Look back at the table at the beginning of this section (**Target point**) and decide on which of the statements you can answer 'Yes' to.

Did you do as well as you expected? Could you improve your work? Use Publisher to add a comment to your work to show what you could do to improve it and remember this when starting your next ICT project.

GET AHEAD

The next project involves making the design for the can. The logo is done of course, but food and drink containers today have to carry much more information than just the name of the food or drink. So have a go at this:

❯❯ Have a look at the packaging for four different items of food and drink.

❯❯ Analyse the use of ICT in the production of the food and drink information (not the actual information, just how it has been done).

❯❯ Fill in the table. To make it really useful in the next lesson, you should include sentences and drawings in your answers, not just ticks or a 'Yes/No' answer.

Food label	Font (size, type)	Layout (table/list)	Use of diagrams (e.g. the 'traffic light' system)

Remember to bring your table and food packaging to your next ICT lesson!

WHAT IT SAYS ON THE TIN

TASK BRIEF

At Design Studio you have just received this email ...

BACKGROUND

The new drink Slurp needs a design for the can. The basics have been done and the style for the brand name Slurp and the colours associated with it have been chosen – but the other information on the label needs to be designed. That's your job!

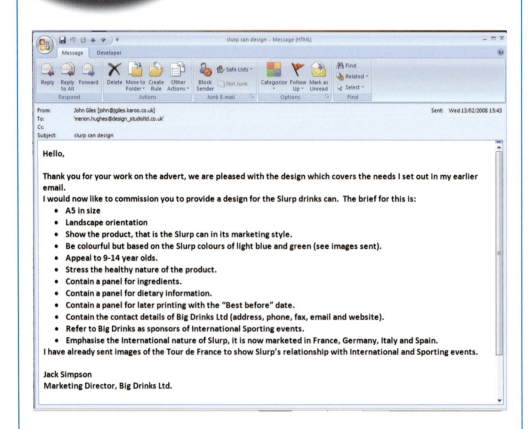

From: John Giles [john@jgiles.karoo.co.uk]
To: 'merion.hughes@design_studioltd.co.uk'
Cc:
Subject: slurp can design

Sent: Wed 13/02/2008 15:43

Hello,

Thank you for your work on the advert, we are pleased with the design which covers the needs I set out in my earlier email.

I would now like to commission you to provide a design for the Slurp drinks can. The brief for this is:

- A5 in size
- Landscape orientation
- Show the product, that is the Slurp can in its marketing style.
- Be colourful but based on the Slurp colours of light blue and green (see images sent).
- Appeal to 9-14 year olds.
- Stress the healthy nature of the product.
- Contain a panel for ingredients.
- Contain a panel for dietary information.
- Contain a panel for later printing with the "Best before" date.
- Contain the contact details of Big Drinks Ltd (address, phone, fax, email and website).
- Refer to Big Drinks as sponsors of International Sporting events.
- Emphasise the International nature of Slurp, it is now marketed in France, Germany, Italy and Spain.

I have already sent images of the Tour de France to show Slurp's relationship with International and Sporting events.

Jack Simpson
Marketing Director, Big Drinks Ltd.

Figure 2.1

SOFTWARE SKILLS

You will learn how to:

> Select page size

> Select page orientation

> Make and use graduated fills

> Crop images

> Make duplicate images

> Combine images

> Layer images

> Group images

FUNCTIONAL SKILLS

As you work through this task the Functional Skills tabs will explain to you why the task tackles the brief in the way shown here and explain why you would choose to:

> Change the page orientation

> Edit images

CAPABILITY

In this task you are learning the skills that will help you to be able to make the appropriate decisions according to the audience and purpose on future projects.

VOCABULARY

You should understand the meaning of these words which may be new to you:

> Template
> Layout
> Orientation
> Portrait
> Landscape
> Navigate
> Crop
> Layer

Always use the spellings we use in Britain in your writing even if you see the US spellings in the software, e.g. use 'colour' and not the US equivalent, 'color'.

RESOURCES

There is only one file for this task:

SlurpAdvert_Template1.pub

You can download these files from www.payne-gallway.co.uk

⊕ TARGET POINT

Turn the page to see your Target Points for this task.

Have a look at the following statements before you start your task so that you know what you are aiming for.

Although you will not make your own decisions on the design of the template in Task 2, you can use what you learn here to help with other work that will be awarded a particular level.

RESOURCES

Level 3	Level 4	Level 5	Level 6
You have saved your work	You have saved your work as a template file		
You have used a new template	You have used the Page Size selection facility		
	You have altered an existing template to fit a new size and orientation		
You have used the cyclist image in your label	You have cropped the cyclist picture correctly		
	You have duplicated the triangle element		
	You have combined triangle elements to make the flag		
	You have used and demonstrated that you understand the use of the group and ungroup tools		
	You have made changes showing that you understand the concept of layering		
		You have made your document suitable for an unfamiliar audience	
	You have used the criteria and met most of the requirements of the brief	You have used the criteria and met all of the requirements of the brief and produced a template appropriate for the target audience	

OK. Let's get started.

Before you start any project, you should organise your folders where you are going to save the work.

In the Publisher folder, create one called **Task2** – this is where you will save the files you will be creating.

The starting point is the template you made for the Slurp advert, but there are some problems with using the advert template for the design for the drinks can.

DESIGNING A LABEL

Read through the email again. Which of the requirements is likely to give us most difficulty when we re-use the advert template?

It's going to be size, isn't it? The advert was **A4** and **Portrait** orientation like this:

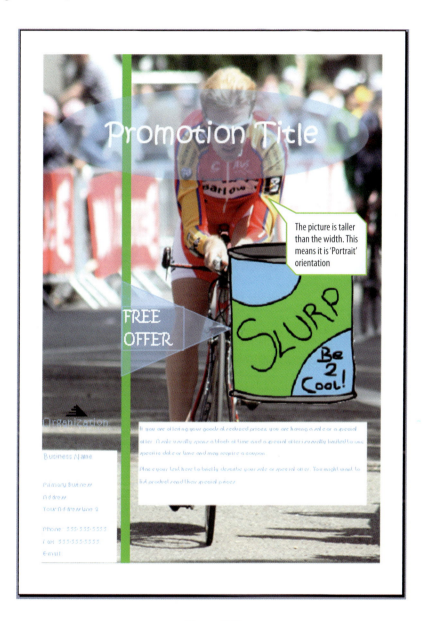

Figure 2.2

But to fit the drinks can we need a label like this:

Figure 2.3

Obviously the advert doesn't match with the size and orientation of the new Slurp can label. We will need to do some work to change the design of the template. It's still worthwhile using the Advert Template, though, because we can re-use most of the objects just by resizing and repositioning them.

Layout

We need to resize and reposition the objects to fit the new page size, but there are another couple of points to remember before we start:

> All of the Slurp logo needs to be visible by looking at the front of the can – it's no use having some of it 'round the back'.

> If Big Drinks are going to market Slurp in other countries, we will need to leave more room for ingredients and dietary information, because some languages will take more room than English.

Here is one possible layout:

Figure 2.4

And here is how to do it:

 Load Publisher 2007.

 Double click the thumbnail image of the advert in the **Recent Publications** pane.

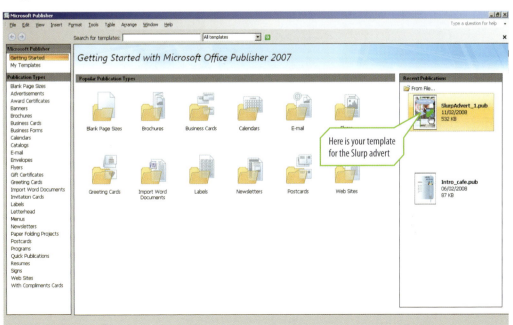

Figure 2.5

Alternatively, look in **My Templates** (in the Tasks pane on the left of the screen) and double click the thumbnail.

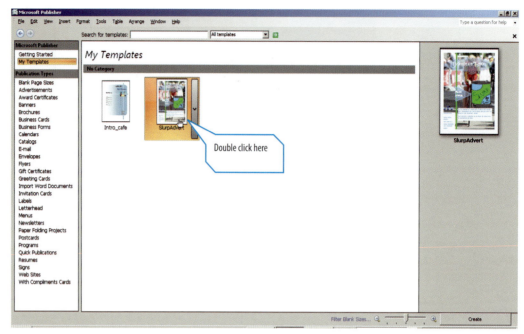

Figure 2.6

Next we need to change the page size.

 Look at the Tasks pane and open the box **Flyer Options** by clicking on the title.

 Click the **Change Page Size** button in the Tasks pane.

SOFTWARE SKILLS
Changing the page size and orientation

Figure 2.7

Choosing the page size

 5 Jack Simpson (Big Drinks Ltd) has asked you to use **A5** size paper and the **Landscape** format (so that the design will wrap round the can). Choose the Blank Page Size shown in Figure 2.8.

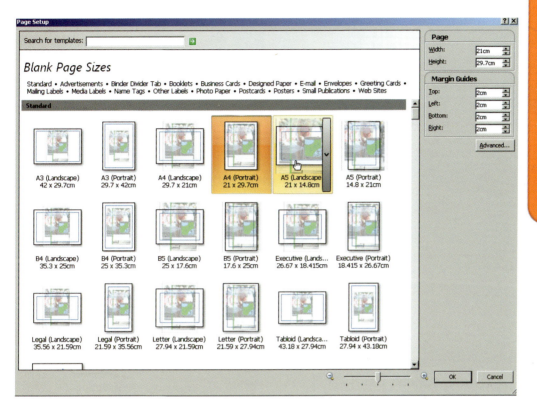

Figure 2.8

 6 Double click the thumbnail for A5 (Landscape).

 7 The view probably does not fit your screen, so adjust the **zoom control** so that you can see all of the objects.

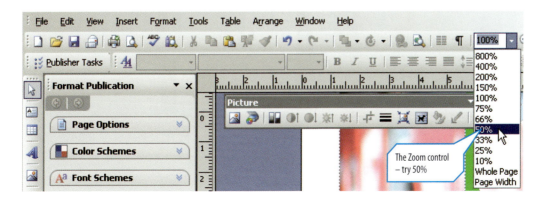

Figure 2.9

FUNCTIONAL SKILLS

Choosing which page orientation (landscape or portrait) to use – in this case we have been asked to use a specific orientation and page size but if this isn't the case you would need to carefully consider whether the choice you made matches your audience and purpose. For example, it would be unusual to use landscape for reports and letters but you could use it for posters and flyers

SOFTWARE SKILLS

Using the zoom control

8 Resize and arrange the objects as in Figure 2.11.

This 'exploded' view shows all of the objects so that you can choose how to arrange them later. Remember to highlight objects before attempting to move or resize them.

TIP
Remember to use the Undo button if it goes horribly wrong!

9 When resizing pictures make sure you only use the corner handles.

Figure 2.10

If you use the handles in the middle of the sides of the picture, you will distort the image. You don't want the cyclist to turn into a sumo wrestler!

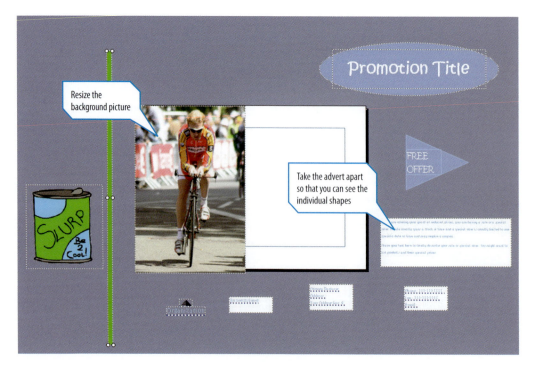

Figure 2.11

SOFTWARE SKILLS

Undoing an action

Resizing an image

Cropping the image

 10 The main problem is fitting the image of the cyclist with that of the Slurp logo. We could make the logo small so that little of the cyclist was obscured, but that would mean the brand was not clearly labelled.

There is some wasted space in the cyclist picture. The area to the left could be removed and this would leave more room for the Slurp logo.

Click on the picture of the cyclist so that it is highlighted.

 11 Look at the **Picture Toolbar** and find the Crop Tool.

 12 Click the **Crop Tool** button.

 13 The handles around the picture turn into dark lines.

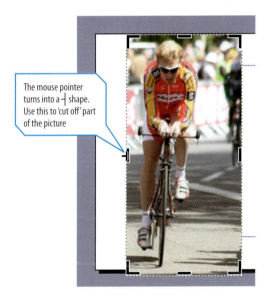

The mouse pointer turns into a ⊣ shape. Use this to 'cut off' part of the picture

Figure 2.12

The mouse pointer changes to a ⊣ shape that you can use to remove part of the left side of the picture.

 14 Click on the **Crop** button again to remove the crop tool from the mouse pointer. (Otherwise you will crop the next picture – chaos!)

 15 Now move the picture to the left and resize the picture to leave a small gap at the top, bottom and the left; I have plans for this space!

The light blue and green colours on the can are striking and memorable. Big Drinks would like people to associate these colours with their drink Slurp. You can probably think of some other examples of this for yourself. We ought to use these colours whenever we can and an obvious opportunity is the background to the can label.

FUNCTIONAL SKILLS

Editing images – when you find a suitable image, think about whether it could look even more effective if you changed it in some way. Here we have chosen to cut (crop) the background so that we can use the best image we have available but also fit it with the other information that we need to fit on the page

SOFTWARE SKILLS

Cropping an image

At present the label is largely white. We'll set about changing that next.

WHAT DO THESE MAKE YOU THINK OF?

> A circle divided into two blue and two white quadrants.

> A tick.

> A bitten apple.

 16 Click **Format** on the menu bar and select **Background**.

TIP

You can also load the Background box into the Tasks pane. Just click the downward pointing arrow and select Background from the list.

Using graduated fills

 17 The **Background** dialogue box loads into the Tasks pane on the left of your screen.

Figure 2.13

SOFTWARE SKILLS
Inserting a background colour

We are going to use both of these colours in a **graduated fill**. This means the blue colour will gradually fade into the green.

 Click on **More Backgrounds**.

The **Fill Effects** dialogue box loads:

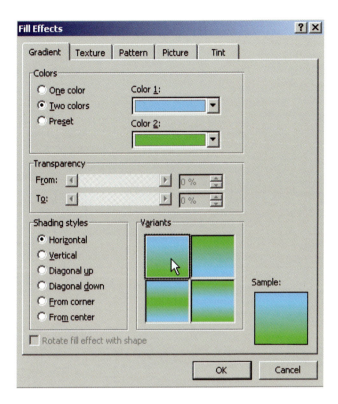

Figure 2.14

 Make the settings that you see in Figure 2.14.

The colours were chosen in a similar way to that which you used in Task 1. (Click the downward pointing arrow in the Color 1 box, select More Colors and then look back at Figure 1.13 in Task 1 on page 22; repeat for Color 2.)

The use of blue at the top and green at the bottom is to contrast with the colour arrangement on the right-hand side of the Slurp can. If the colours were the other way round, the colours would match and the logo would merge into the background.

 Click **OK**.

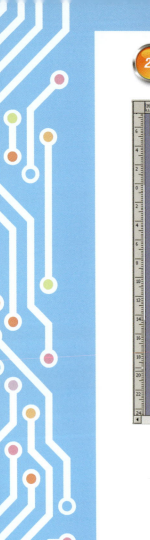

21 Arrange the Slurp can next to the cyclist and adjust its size:

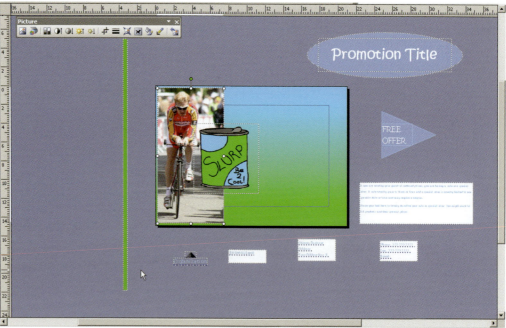

Figure 2.15

Now the cyclist has a narrow border at the top, bottom and left-hand side and the Slurp can is prominent.

Remember we have about half of the label to use for the 'front' of the label. If we use more than half, part of it will curve round and be at the back of the can.

It's time to look back at Jack Simpson's email and see how many of his requirements we have covered so far.

Hmm, not bad; we seem to have covered some of the bases, but the international and sporting links are not there yet. Let's see if we can satisfy both of these requirements together because we don't have much room. We will use the triangle shape for this.

Ungrouping

22 Before we start, there is an idea that you need to have in mind. The triangle is made from two shapes – that's why you can see an inner rectangle.

At the moment these shapes are linked together. This is called grouping and is the reason why we can't separate them using just the mouse. We will **Ungroup** them and delete the rectangle.

Delete the writing.

23 Make sure the triangle is highlighted, then click on **Arrange** on the menu bar and select **Ungroup** from the drop-down menu.

 24 Both objects will be highlighted but we want to separate out the rectangular text box. First of all, remove the highlighting by clicking anywhere off the triangle and rectangle.

 25 Now click on the edge of the rectangle and drag it clear of the triangle – we will use this later.

Copying

 26 You are going to transform the triangle into a picture of the French flag, the tricolour. This will need three triangles superimposed, one partly overlapping on the other. Let's copy the triangle first.

Make sure that the triangle is highlighted and has eight white handles around its edge (there are two yellow and one green as well, but don't worry about these).

 27 Hold down the **Ctrl** key (bottom left of your keyboard) and press **C**.

 28 Now hold down the **Ctrl** key again and this time Press **V**.

Another copy of the triangle arrives!

 29 Hold down the **Ctrl** key and press **V** again.

30 Now you've got three copies of the triangle!

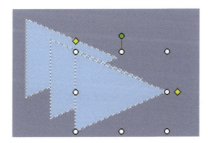

Figure 2.16

Colouring AutoShapes

 31 To colour the triangles in the colours of the French flag, click on one of the triangles to select it and then right click and choose **Format AutoShape** from the shortcut menu.

The Format AutoShape dialogue box opens.

SOFTWARE SKILLS

Copying and pasting

Colouring shapes

32 Swap to the **Colors and Lines** tab.

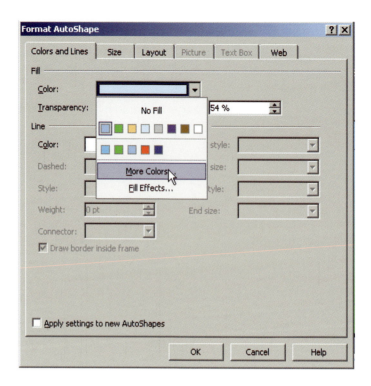

Figure 2.17

33 Click the inverted triangle to open the Color options and select **More Colors**. The **Colors** palette loads.

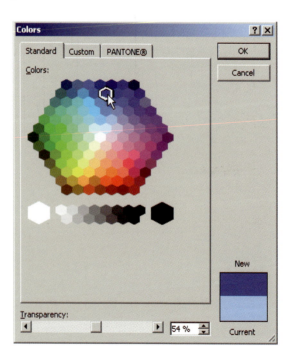

Figure 2.18

Select a strong blue colour for the first part of the flag and click **OK**.

 Make sure that the **Transparency** control is set to zero and then click **OK**.

One blue triangle!

 Do the same for the other two triangles, colouring one white and the other a bright red.

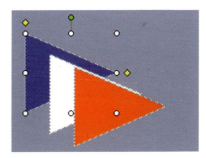

Figure 2.19

This makes quite a nice shape, but it might be better if we make a single triangle by putting one triangle on top of another so that we have three layers of triangles. There is an obvious problem with this; all three triangles are exactly the same size, so they will not make a tricolour flag. We need to reduce the size of the white and red triangles.

 Resize the white and red triangles.

 Re-align the white and red triangles so that they fit together.

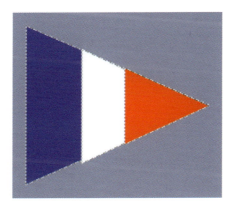

Figure 2.20

TIP

You can move the triangles to line them up accurately by highlighting a triangle and then using the cursor keys (the ones with arrows on them at the bottom right of your keyboard).

Grouping

 There is going to be a problem with our new triangular flag. If you try to move it, it will come to bits again: all that lining up will have to be done again.

Thankfully, there is a way round this problem and it is the reverse of the Ungrouping you did earlier. First of all, you need to select *all three* of the triangles.

Click on the left edge of the blue triangle to select it and then hold down the Ctrl key.

 Click on the left edge of the white triangle. You will notice that the mouse pointer has now a '+' sign next to it to show it is adding to the selection.

SOFTWARE SKILLS
Grouping objects

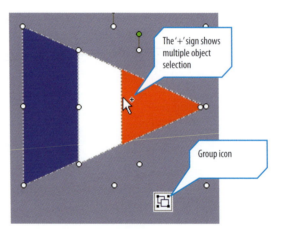

The '+' sign shows multiple object selection

Group icon

Figure 2.21

 When you have selected all three triangles, click on the **Group** icon (see Figure 2.21).

Notice that now there is only one set of handles. Try moving the shape – the three triangles move as one!

Even better, try resizing the shape – the shape behaves as one rather than three separate triangles.

Layers

 You can now put that text box to good use.

Choose a suitable font and font size. Then type in 'Sponsors of the Tour de France' into the text box.

 Now drag the text box over the triangular flag.

Wow! Where's it gone?

The problem is to do with layers again; the text box is a bottom layer and has 'slid underneath' the upper layers of the flag.

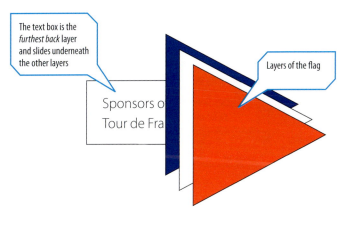

Figure 2.22

SOFTWARE SKILLS
Using layers

We need to use **Bring to Front** to make the text box the top layer.

 Highlight the text box and then click on the **Arrange** icon on the menu bar.

 Select **Order** and then **Bring to Front** in the sub-menu.

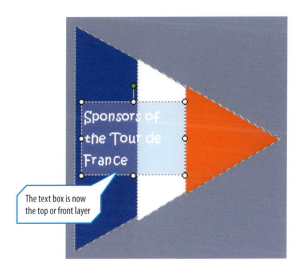

Figure 2.23

Finishing touches

 There is still the problem that the colour of the text box interferes with the colours of the flag.

Right click on the text box and choose **Format Text Box** from the shortcut menu.

The Format Text Box dialogue box appears.

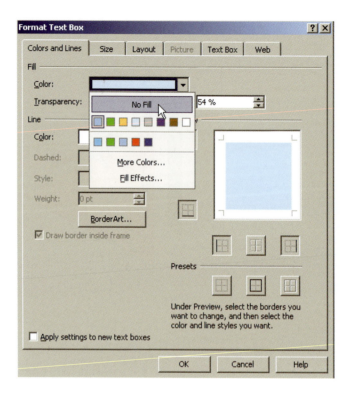

Figure 2.24

 In the **Color** box select **No Fill** (see Figure 2.24).

Change the font colour so that it shows up over the colours of the flag.

 Click **Format** on the menu bar and select **Font**.

The Font dialogue box loads. Here you can change the font type, its size and colour:

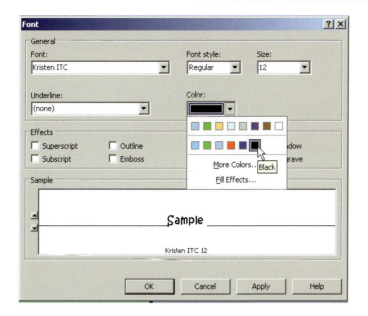

Figure 2.25

49 Now highlight the text and use the **Center** tool on the **Formatting** toolbar to centre the text in the text box.

50 Finally **Group** the text box with the flag shape.

51 Move the completed flag over the label and position it as in Figure 2.26.

52 Click on the Slurp can shape and **Bring to Front**.

You should now have a label looking something like this:

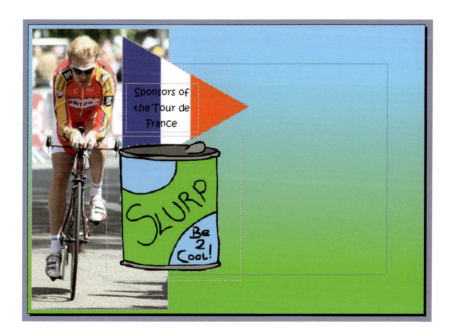

Figure 2.26

53 The name of the organisation 'Big Drinks Ltd' needs to be placed on the label; you can put this at the bottom right.

54 And lastly, the 'Dietary information' and 'Ingredients' text boxes can be resized and placed in position as in Figure 2.27.

We haven't any information for these boxes yet, so just leave them blank until Big Drinks tell us what they want us to type into the boxes.

That just leaves the green line, a text box and the 'Promotions' box. I couldn't use the 'Promotions' box so I deleted it, but the text box has become the 'Best Before Date' box and the green line I have positioned to the left of the cyclist because I felt it made an effective border.

Figure 2.27

55 Give the label a final look over, checking that the text is spelt correctly and the text boxes are aligned correctly.

56 Click **File** and select **Save As**.

Saving as a template

 57 We may have another project from Big Drinks and perhaps would be able to use this as a template, so it would be best to save this in the templates folder.

Open the box **Save as type** and select **Publisher Template**.

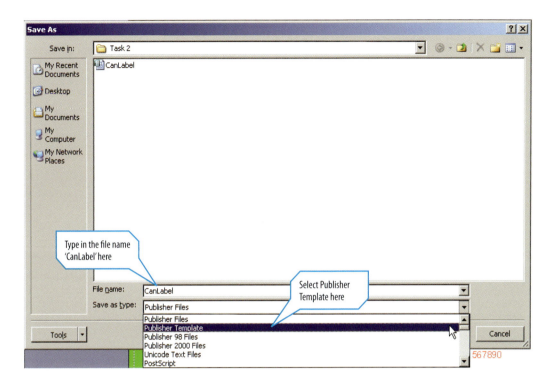

Figure 2.28

ALL DONE

That's it – we can send it off to Big Drinks Ltd again for their approval!

Big Drinks go international!

There are a few things that you could do to extend the project.

You may be studying a language or two, so why not show your language skills and produce another template in that language?

You could use the same template as a starting point but change the organisation that Big Drinks are sponsoring to another one – like Sport Relief, which helps people around the world through sponsorship for getting fit. You might think of another one but remember to match the aims of the company with whom you choose to sponsor.

CHECKPOINT

Check that you know how to:

> Select a page size.

> Select a template.

> Save a template.

> Use the Zoom control.

> Navigate to find a file.

> Crop a picture.

> Place a picture in a Publisher document.

> Resize a picture without distortion.

> Resize a text box and picture frame.

> Delete a text box and picture frame.

> Format a picture: fill colour, transparency.

> Use a graduated fill.

> Use keyboard shortcuts to copy and paste.

> Combine shapes to make a more complex image.

> Group and Ungroup objects.

> Use the Order control to move images to the back and forwards to alter their visibility in the finished document.

ASSESSMENT POINT

Now let's assess the work. Look back at the table at the beginning of this section (**Target point**) and decide on which of the statements you can answer 'Yes' to.

Did you do as well as you expected? Could you improve your work? Use Publisher to add a comment to your work to show what you could do to improve it and remember this when starting your next ICT project.

GET AHEAD

In the next project you will learn how to send a personal letter to many people. This sounds easy, but it requires lots of work. It is easy once you know how, but it doesn't require much extra work because we can get the computer to help us.

To prepare for this, collect about six letters that have been sent to your family as 'mail shots'. Mail shots are usually a way of advertising a service or a product such as double glazing or offering to build a conservatory. Choose letters where the sender seems to know your family and uses a personal name in the 'salutation'; in other words:

Dear Mr Smith

… or even:

Dear James,

… and not:

Dear Sir.

Look at the ways the letters have been made personal to your family and then complete this table:

Letter (type of letter or type of sender)	Example of a personalised item	Example of a non-personalised item	Advantages of personalising	Disadvantages of personalising

SPREADING THE NEWS

TASK BRIEF

At Design Studio you have just received this email …

BACKGROUND

Big Drinks need to tell retailers (shops and supermarkets) about Slurp and the competition they have set up. They want to use email to do this Your job is to make an attractive design for the email and ensure that it looks like a personal message from Jack Simpson, the Marketing Director at Big Drinks Ltd who you have been doing some work for over the past few weeks.

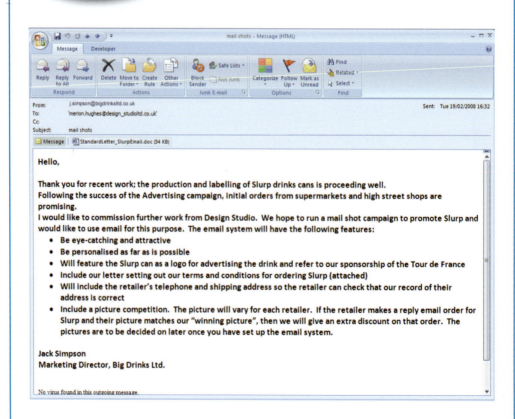

mail shots - Message (HTML)

From:	j.simpson@bigdrinksltd.co.uk	Sent:	Tue 19/02/2008 16:32
To:	'merion.hughes@design_studioltd.co.uk'		
Cc:			
Subject:	mail shots		

Message   StandardLetter_SlurpEmail.doc (34 KB)

Hello,

Thank you for recent work; the production and labelling of Slurp drinks cans is proceeding well.
Following the success of the Advertising campaign, initial orders from supermarkets and high street shops are promising.
I would like to commission further work from Design Studio. We hope to run a mail shot campaign to promote Slurp and would like to use email for this purpose. The email system will have the following features:

- Be eye-catching and attractive
- Be personalised as far as is possible
- Will feature the Slurp can as a logo for advertising the drink and refer to our sponsorship of the Tour de France
- Include our letter setting out our terms and conditions for ordering Slurp (attached)
- Will include the retailer's telephone and shipping address so the retailer can check that our record of their address is correct
- Include a picture competition. The picture will vary for each retailer. If the retailer makes a reply email order for Slurp and their picture matches our "winning picture", then we will give an extra discount on that order. The pictures are to be decided on later once you have set up the email system.

Jack Simpson
Marketing Director, Big Drinks Ltd.

No virus found in this outgoing message.

Figure 3.1

SOFTWARE SKILLS

You will learn how to:

> Navigate a file and folder structure

> Work systematically by grouping assets for a task

> Use and modify WordArt

> Make and use a simple database

> Import data

> Select destinations for data

FUNCTIONAL SKILLS

As you work through this task the Functional Skills tabs will explain to you why the task tackles the brief in the way shown here and explain why you would choose to:

> Combine different types of information

> Use text boxes

> Use bullet points

> Use email

> Use a database

CAPABILITY

In this task you are learning the skills that will help you to be able to make the appropriate decisions according to the audience and purpose on future projects.

VOCABULARY

You should understand the meaning of these words which may be new to you:

> Template

> Layout

> Navigate

> Database

> Standard Letter

> Email

> E-Mail Merge

> Database field

> Place holder

Always use the spellings we use in Britain in your writing even if you see the US spellings in the software, e.g. use 'colour' and not the US equivalent, 'color'.

RESOURCES

These are the files for this task:

StandardLetter_ SlurpEmail.doc

SlurpCan_ 1.jpg

The 'Tour de France' triangle made in Task 2

Image1.jpg Image2.jpg, Image3.jpg and Image4.jpg

You can download these files from www.payne-gallway.co.uk

TARGET POINT

Turn the page to see your Target Points for this task.

TARGET POINT

Have a look at the following statements before you start your task so that you know what you are aiming for.

Although you will not make your own decisions on the design of the email layout and formatting in Task 3, you can use what you learn here to help with other work that will be awarded a particular level.

Level 3	Level 4	Level 5	Level 6
You have saved your work	You have saved your work in an appropriate folder	You have set up a folder structure to help you to work in a systematic manner	
You have arranged some of the files that you need	You have found and relocated the files you will need	You have shown a methodical approach: arranging files in a new folder and other needed files in the Content Library	
You can create the body of an email	You have used the E-mail Merge wizard tool to make a personalised email for several recipients	You recognise the need to check the size of the file attached	
		You have set up the database and imported all of the fields into the correct locations in the Standard Letter	You understand the advantages of the email system that makes use of a database studied in Task 3 and an example of when it would be used
You have used a new template	You have used the Style controls to modify an existing template including changes to show that you understand layering		
	You have combined different forms of information into your document and styled it appropriately for your audience		
		You have made your document suitable for an unfamiliar audience	
	You have used the criteria and met most of the requirements of the brief	You have used the criteria and met all of the requirements of the brief and produced a template appropriate for the target audience	

OK. Let's get started.

Before you start any project, you should organise your folders where you are going to save the work.

In the Publisher folder, create one called **Task3** – this is where you will save the files you will be creating.

How E-Mail Merge works

The idea of E-mail Merge is to save time by sending the same email to a lot of different people, but still making it feel personal by changing certain details such as the recipient's name, e.g. 'Dear Mr Jones'. There are two parts to this system:

❯ a 'Standard Letter', which in our case will be in the email.

❯ a database, which will contain a list of the names and addresses of the shops and supermarkets.

The system works by having the gaps in the email for the names and addresses filled by the names and addresses in the database. So although you have only written one email, you will be sending it to as many people as the addresses you have in your database. Some companies use this system to send out thousands of emails at a time. You can see how the system works here:

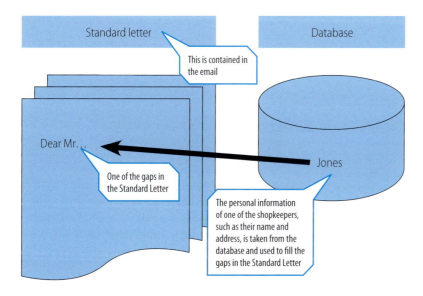

Figure 3.2

Template

Load Publisher and have a look at the variety of E-mail templates in the left-hand Tasks pane listed under **Publication Types**.

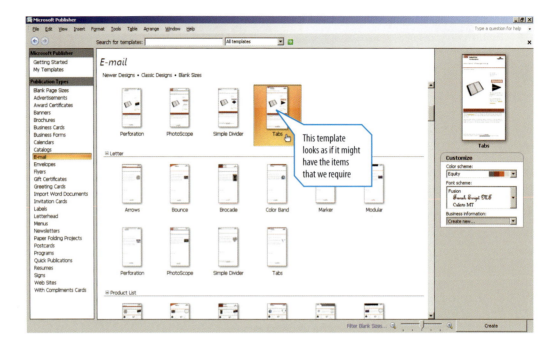

Figure 3.3

FUNCTIONAL SKILLS

Combining information types – here we are trying to attract the attention of customers to encourage them to buy the new drink Slurp. We need to create an advert that is eye-catching but also provides them with all the information they need, so we are using a combination of images and text. There are lots of different parts to the advert, so we are using a template that will help us to organise our information into text and image boxes. We can arrange them easily on the page and find the most attractive but useful layout

The Tabs template looks as if it has most of the items we will need such as:

➤ A text box for the Standard Letter.

➤ A graphic (an image or picture) that we can change for the picture of the Slurp can, which will become the logo.

➤ A triangular shape, which we have used in both the advert and the label.

➤ Text boxes, which we can use for the contact details of the shop or supermarket.

➤ A text box for the price of Slurp orders.

➤ Space for the competition picture.

➤ Text box for the company (Big Drinks Ltd) name and logo.

➤ Text box for the name 'Slurp'.

➤ Text box for Big Drinks email address.

It's important for companies like Big Drinks to use a logo because the logo acts as a 'mental shortcut', making the viewer recognise the product even without reading its name. We have established the Slurp can as the logo for the Big Drinks product Slurp in the advert (Task 1) and the can label (Task 2), so we must use exactly the same picture as the logo in this E-mail Merge.

E-MAIL MERGE
Content Library

 Before you start, have a look the resources that you will need (listed on page 59) and insert them in the Content Library so that you have the resources to hand and won't have to hunt them down later on.

To copy the Tour de France triangle, open the can label from Task 2 and highlight the triangle.

 Change the Tasks pane so that it shows the Content Library (there will be other items in the library from Task 1).

 Click **Add selected items to Content Library** (in blue text at the bottom of the Tasks pane).

The Tour de France triangle appears as a thumbnail in the Content Library (see Figure 3.4).

SOFTWARE SKILLS

Adding assets to content library

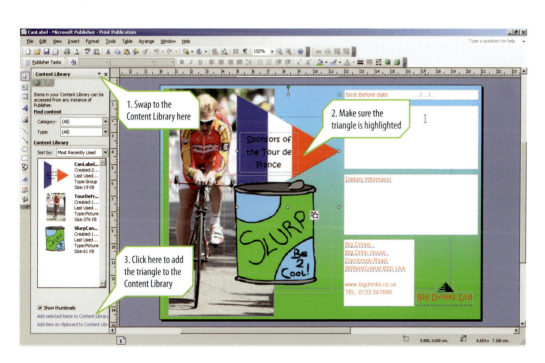

Figure 3.4

Repeat this if you need to add the image of the Slurp can to the Content Library.

 To add the Standard Letter to the Content Library, navigate to the folder containing the Standard Letter. The file you want is called StandardLetter_SlurpEmail.

The Standard Letter has two parts: the writing and Jack Simpson's signature.

Both of these need to be added to the Content Library so that they are ready for you to use later on.

5 Double click the file. It will open in Publisher (see Figure 3.5).

6 Swap to the Content Library in the Tasks pane.

7 Click **Add selected items to Content Library** (select the **Business** category as before).

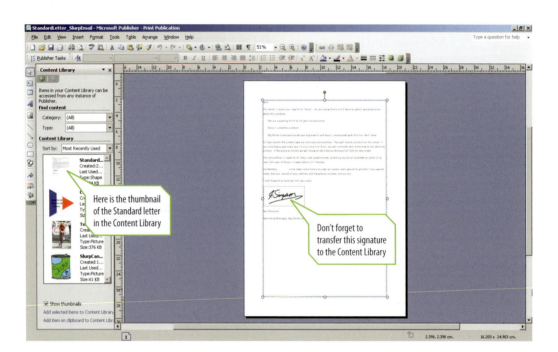

Figure 3.5

8 Highlight the signature and add this to the Content Library.

9 Click **File** on the menu bar and select **Close** to close the Standard Letter file. Repeat this to close the label from Task 2.

You are now back to the original **Getting Started** screen showing the templates.

Layout

We need to be cautious about the amount of colour and pictures that we use in the design of the email because both of these will affect its size and speed.

If we make the email too large, it will take a long time for shops to download. They will get fed up and not bother with the email, probably just deleting it to save time and space on their computer.

10 Double click the thumbnail of the Tabs template so that it loads into the main window of Publisher.

We'll start by changing the colour scheme used in the email. It would be useful to be able to use the Slurp green and blue colours throughout the email.

 11 Swap to **Color Schemes** in the Tasks pane.

 12 Select the colour scheme that you made in Task 1 called **SlurpCan_AdvertScheme**.

Unfortunately, the new template does not use the colour scheme very well. Look at the bar at the top of the email – it's a mucky brown rather than green!

Let's change the scheme so that the colours apply to important objects in the email.

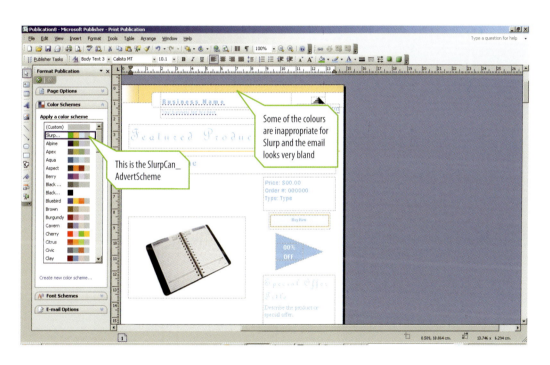

Figure 3.6

 13 Right click on SlurpCan_AdvertScheme in the Color Schemes pane and choose **Edit Scheme** from the shortcut menu.

We need to change the light brown used in the bar at the top of the email to the green used in the Slurp can. Look at the **Edit Color Scheme** dialogue box. You can see that Accent 1 is currently showing the 'Slurp Green' colour:

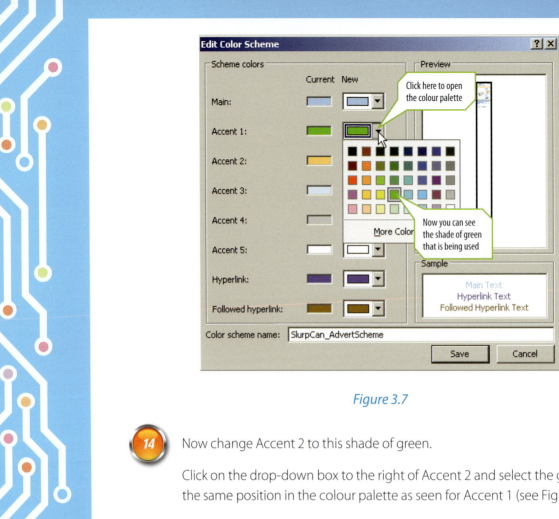

Figure 3.7

14 Now change Accent 2 to this shade of green.

Click on the drop-down box to the right of Accent 2 and select the green from the same position in the colour palette as seen for Accent 1 (see Figure 3.8).

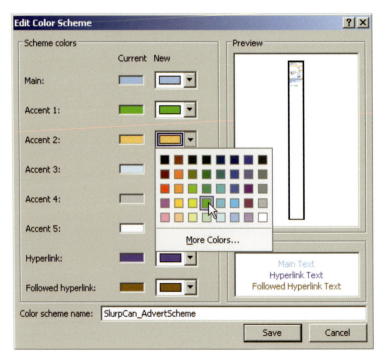

Figure 3.8

15 Now make a new folder called **SlurpEmailMerge** and save your publisher file in it using the filename **SlurpEmail**.

There are some picture files that will be needed later – so while we have the new folder in mind, it is best to navigate to these and save a copy of them in your new SlurpEmailMerge folder so that they are handy for later on. The files you need are: **Image1.jpg**, **Image2.jpg**, **Image3.jpg** and **Image4.jpg**.

The work on colours has made an improvement, but we will need to do some more work to make the email relevant to Slurp and have more visual impact.

Next job is to change the existing picture to a small picture of the Slurp can which we will use as a logo.

 16 Highlight and then press the **Delete** key to remove the picture of the open book.

 17 Swap to the **Content Library** in the Tasks pane.

 18 Click on the image of the Slurp can and drag it onto the email template.

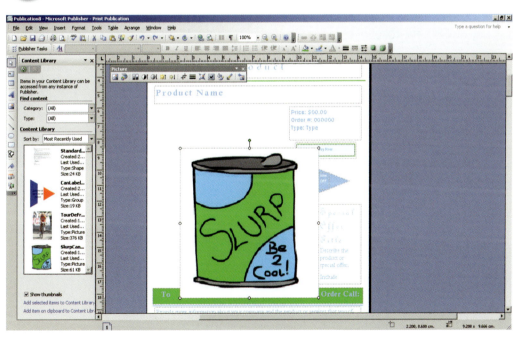

Figure 3.9

 19 Resize and reposition the Slurp image. Remember it doesn't need to be large; there is no need for detail – the image is acting as a logo, not a picture of what a real can would look like.

TIP

Remember to use the corner handles when resizing a picture to avoid it becoming too thin or fat.

The triangle shape is not adding to the impact of the email, so we will change this for the Tour de France triangle – another good example of how a computer can save doing lots of work by re-using something that took ages to make in the first place!

 20 Drag the Tour de France triangle from the Content Library to the email.

That's the basic layout completed. It's best to save your work again now before you start formatting.

 21 Make a folder and in it save your file as **SlurpEmail**.

Formatting the layout

First of all, it's time to do a little tidying. With the clutter of unneeded text boxes it is difficult to work!

 22 Delete the following text boxes:

> 'Business name'

> 'Your business tag line here'

> 'Featured Product'

> 'Product Name'

> 'Buy Now'

> '00% OFF'

FUNCTIONAL SKILLS

Using textboxes – by putting our information into text and image boxes, we can move them around the page and from our content library by dragging and dropping them into place. This makes the process simpler than copying and pasting

TIP

It is easier to keep track of these deletions if you drag them off the email template and then delete them.

If you get completely mixed up, remember the undo button!

Hmm, that's better – the email doesn't look so cluttered now. If we had left all of the text boxes in place the reader would have been distracted from the important information.

The triangle and Slurp can could make a good group in a similar way to that in the label. What we now are missing is a good title for the email; it should have the name 'Slurp' and we could improve on ordinary text by using WordArt.

 23 Click on the **WordArt** button  on the **Objects** toolbar on the left of the Tasks pane.

The **WordArt Gallery** dialogue box loads. It's tempting to look for the most wacky WordArt style – resist! Select the one shown. We can make this interesting and fit with Slurp's themes later.

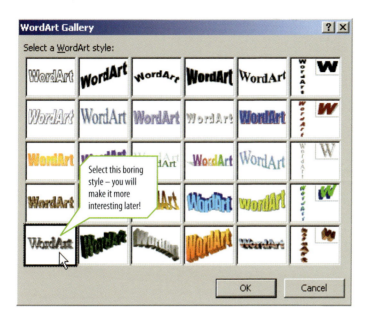

Figure 3.10

 24 Double click your selection.

 25 The **Edit WordArt** dialogue box loads.

 26 Type 'SLURP' (in capital letters) where it says Your Text Here.

Change the font to a more casual style than the default Times New Roman. Remember that the product is supposed to be targeted at 9–14-year-olds and the title should reflect this, while remaining legible for the benefit of the reader!

In this example we have used Kristen ITC font, size 36, typeset Bold (see Figure 3.14), but you could make your own choice. After all, you are the age of the target group and may well be better qualified than me to choose a suitable font!

 27 Click **OK**.

The WordArt shape loads, but we could improve the colour.

Look at the 'floating' WordArt toolbar and click the **Format WordArt** button.

Figure 3.11

The Format WordArt dialogue box loads.

 Swap to the **Colors and Lines** tab.

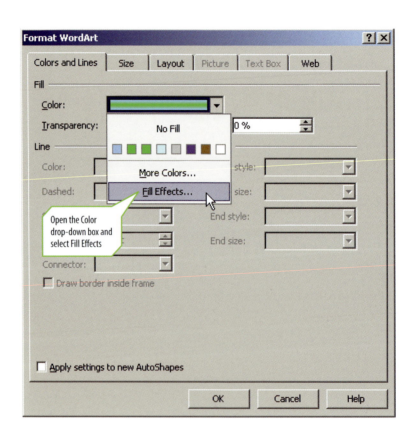

Figure 3.12

30 Select **Fill Effects** as shown in Figure 3.13.

The Fill Effects dialogue box loads.

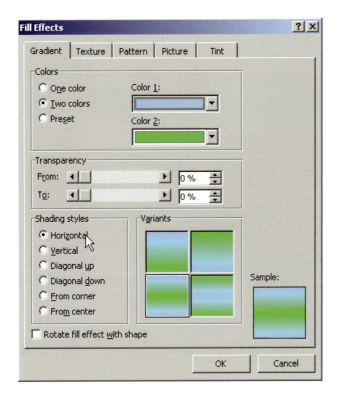

Figure 3.13

31 Select two colours in the Color pane.

32 For **Color 1**, select a colour matching the blue used for the Slurp can.

33 For **Color 2**, select a colour matching the green used for the Slurp can.

34 In the **Shading Styles** pane select the radio button for **Horizontal**.

35 Click **OK** and then **OK** on the Format WordArt dialogue box.

36 Move the WordArt title to its position as shown in Figure 3.14.

Figure 3.14

The Standard Letter

37 Delete the writing in the 'Provide more information' text box.

38 Drag the Standard Letter from the Content Library and drop it in the now empty text box.

Oh dear, it doesn't look great!

The text is light blue and almost unreadable. To make things worse, the formatting is horrible and the writing does not all fit in the text box.

You need to solve these problems next. Start with moving the text boxes under the one we are using (look out for the very thin one); this will give you sufficient room to lengthen the text box for the Standard Letter. Highlight the boxes (use the Ctrl key to allow you to highlight both) then use the down arrowed cursor key to move the boxes together down the page.

39 Highlight the text and click **Format** on the menu bar.

40 Select **Font** from the drop-down menu and use the Font dialogue box to set the Font to Arial, Bold size 12, colour Black. You may see a tick in Superscript – if it's there, click to remove it.

FUNCTIONAL SKILLS

Choosing a font – the font type and size chosen for the letter is suitable for our audience because it is clear, looks formal and professional, and is a standard font used for many business letters

41 Click **OK**.

42 Drag the Jack Simpson's signature from the Content Library and reposition it above his name (see Figure 3.15).

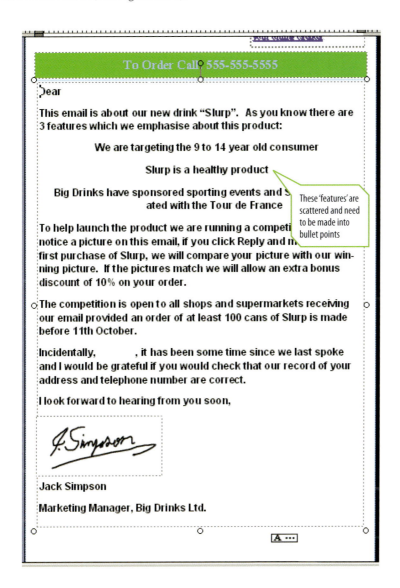

Figure 3.15

43 The features are scattered, so we will attend to these next.

Highlight the 'features' and click the **Align Text Left** button  on the Formatting toolbar.

SOFTWARE SKILLS

Aligning text

Adding bullets

FUNCTIONAL SKILLS

Bullet points – we have used bullet points to emphasise certain parts of the text and make it stand out from the rest. It is always worthwhile highlighting the most important parts of your message so that your audience's eye is drawn to them. Bullets and numbering are the most appropriate ways of highlighting several points in a letter

44 Now put the bullet points back by clicking the **Bullets** button on the Formatting toolbar.

We'll make the place for the competition picture next.

45 Change the text in the 'Special Offer' text box to 'Competition Picture'. It's probably easier to delete the box and start again with this one – the text box tool is on the **Objects** toolbar just to the left of the Tasks pane.

SOFTWARE SKILLS

Sending an email

FUNCTIONAL SKILLS

Using email – the advert is being emailed because it is the fastest, cheapest and most convenient way to reach the customers, and it makes it easy for them to reply with their orders for Slurp

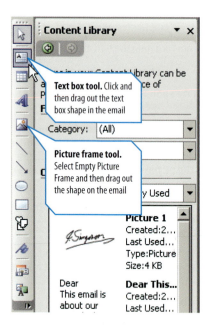

Figure 3.16

46 Make the picture frame as shown in Figure 3.17.

 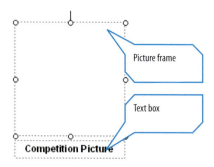

Figure 3.17

Drag the 'Price' text box into place and replace the text as you see in Figure 3.18.

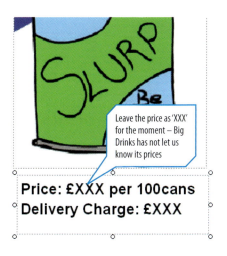

Figure 3.18

Looking again at the logo, I thought it might be fun to make the 'Slurp' name look as if it is coming out of the can and add some bubbles:

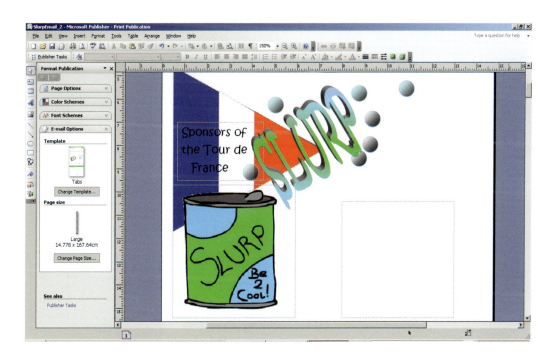

Figure 3.19

To make the 'Slurp' name slope, click on the shape and use the special handle to rotate it so that it is in line with the lower edge of the triangle.

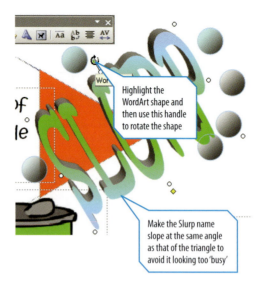

Figure 3.20

 One of the AutoShapes on the **Objects** toolbar was used to make the bubbles; you could use the **Oval** shape for this purpose.

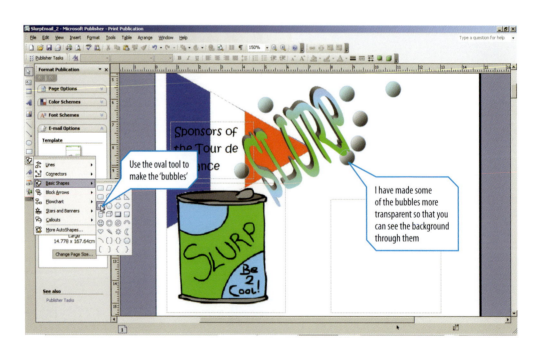

Figure 3.21

 Format the bubble by right clicking and selecting **Format AutoShapes**.

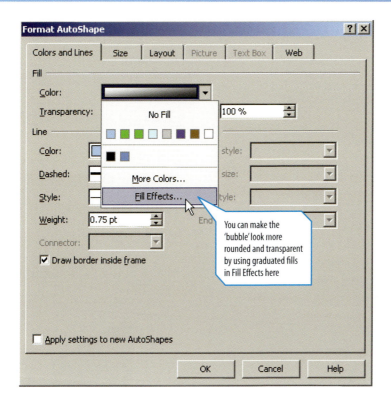

Figure 3.22

51 Make one bubble and then use Ctrl-C to copy it and Ctrl-V to paste a number of copies.

As you can see in Figure 3.21, using the Format AutoShapes dialogue box it is possible to make the bubbles appear transparent.

52 Type 'Big Drinks Ltd' into the 'Organisation' box and format the writing to make it legible.

In the 'Questions or comments' box change the text to:

> **Please reply with your order to:**
> **bigdrinksltd.co.uk**

53 Format the writing so that it is legible.

54 Make a new text box for Big Drinks' contact details and position it in the space above the logo.

55 Type in the contact details:

> **Big Drinks House, Cheslyn Hay, Cannock, Staffs., ST50 1AA**
> **TEL: 01234 567891**
> **www.bigdrinksltd.co.uk**

56 Save your work.

E-Mail Merge

 57 You could send the email now by selecting **Send E-mail** from the **File** menu on the menu bar.

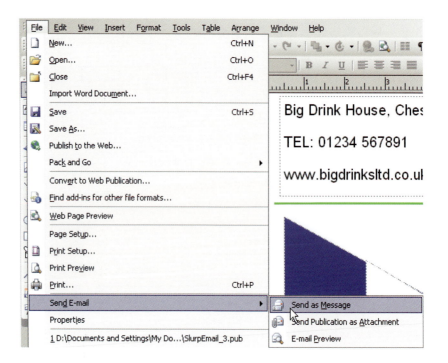

Figure 3.23

 58 Select **Send as Message**.

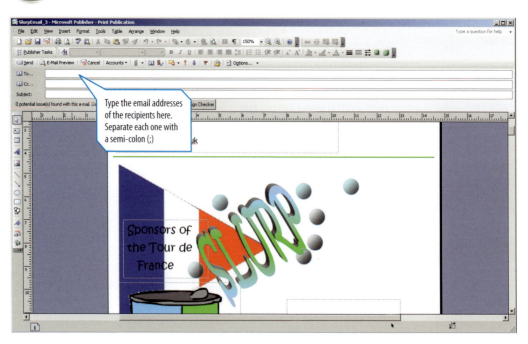

Figure 3.24

If you type the email address of the recipient in the To box, the email will be sent to that person. To send the email to more people you would need to write all of their email addresses in the To box, each separated from the next by a semi-colon.

This is probably the best method if you only want to send this email once, but Big Drinks may send this, or a very similar email, to the same shops several times.

You can see that this will involve a lot of work, especially if there are thousands of shops! There must be an easier way … and, of course, using a computer, we can usually find a way to reduce the amount of work that we need to do. This is where E-mail Merge comes in.

 Click the **Cancel** button to return to the Normal view.

Figure 3.25

 Make sure that the Tasks pane is visible. If it is missing, you can replace it from the **View** drop-down menu.

 Select **E-mail Merge** in the Tasks pane.

Figure 3.26

The E-mail Merge wizard loads.

Step 1

 Make the setting as shown in Figure 3.27, then click on **Next**.

FUNCTIONAL SKILLS

Creating a database – putting the names and email addresses of the customers into a database makes it very easy to edit if we want to add or delete names later on, or send another email to all or part of the list of addresses. We don't have to keep re-typing new lists

SOFTWARE SKILLS

Creating a database

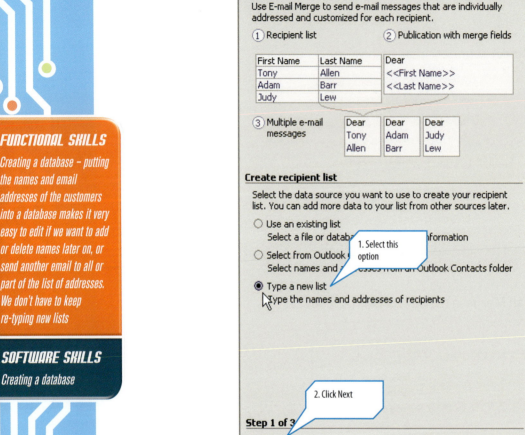

Figure 3.27

The **New Address List** dialogue box arrives.

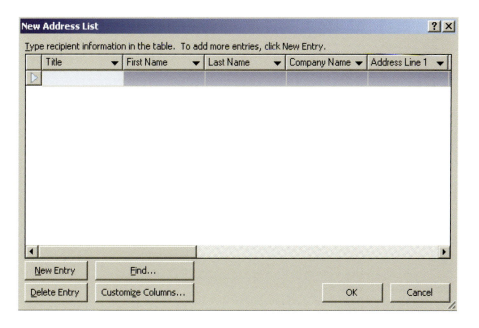

Figure 3.28

 We need to change the columns in the Address List to suit our own email.

Click **Customize Columns**.

Figure 3.29

It's obvious that some of these Columns (or Field Names, as they are more correctly named) are not useful to us – let's remove them first.

64 Delete the following Field Names:

> State.

> Home Phone.

ZIP Code is the American equivalent of the post code used in Britain.

65 Click on **ZIP Code**.

66 Click the **Rename** button.

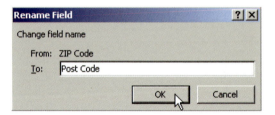

Figure 3.30

67 Change the field name to 'Post Code'.

68 Click **OK**.

69 You need to add another column for the competition pictures.

Click **Add**.

70 In the Add Field dialogue box, type in 'Picture'.

71 Click **OK**.

72 Use the **Move Down** button to move the Picture Field Name to the bottom of the list.

73 Click **OK** on the Customize Address List dialogue box.

74 Click in the blank space under Title and type 'Mr'.

75 Click in the next column (First Name) and type 'John'.

Title	First name	Last name	Company name	Address line 1	Address line 2	City	Post code	Country	Work phone	Email	Competition picture
Mr	John	Green	Green's Greens	221 High Street	Essingford	Stafford	ST50 1AB	UK	01234 567890	greens@greens.co.uk	Image1.jpg
Mrs	Sally	Black	Black's Super Saver	437 Beverley Rd	Erewash	Derby	DE50 1BB	UK	02345 678901	sally@blackssupersaver.co.uk	Image2.jpg
Mdm	Claire	Rouge	Magasin Rouge	Rue des Oiseaux	Rennes le Chateau	Annecy	751234	France	+331234 567890	rouge@rouge.free.fr	Image3.jpg
Mr	Greg	Brown	Brown's Corner	23 North Gate	Holm	York	YO50 1AA	UK	03456 789012	greg@dutchy.co.uk	Image4.jpg

> **TIP**
> Notice the 'File Extensions' in the Competition picture column (.jpg) and don't forget the dot! These need to be typed into the Address List dialogue box.

76 Now type in the rest of the shopkeepers' contact details. You will need to click the **New Entry** button after adding each shopkeeper's details.

77 When you have added all of the recipients, click **OK**.

78 Click **Yes** in the 'Do you want to update your recipient list and save these changes…' box.

You will be returned to the Mail Merge Recipients dialogue box, where you can check that the entries are correct:

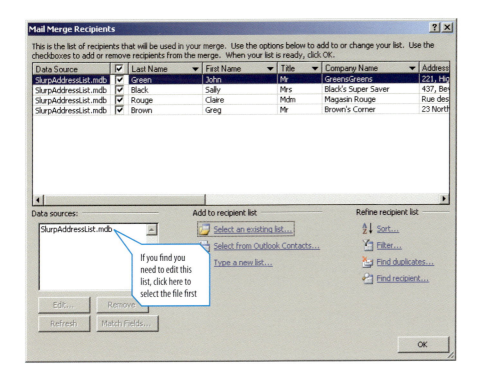

Figure 3.31

TIP

If you have to go back and edit the list in this dialogue box, click the name of the file first in the Data Sources pane; then click the Edit button.

 79 Click **Next** (towards the bottom of the Tasks pane).

Step 2

 80 In this step we link the items in the Recipient List (the database) with the Standard Letter. An additional job is to show where each of the items such as First Name or the Address is to go in the email.

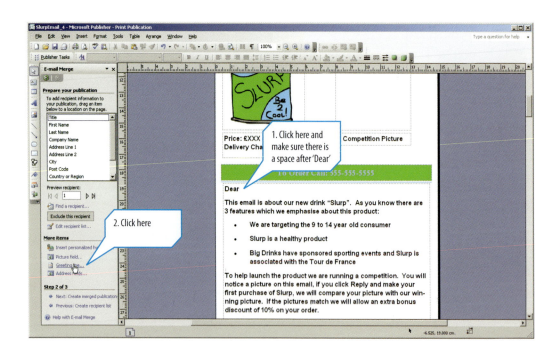

Figure 3.32

81 Click where the 'salutation' (the 'Dear Mr Green') is to go in the email. Have a look at Figure 3.33.

The **Insert Greeting Line** dialogue box loads.

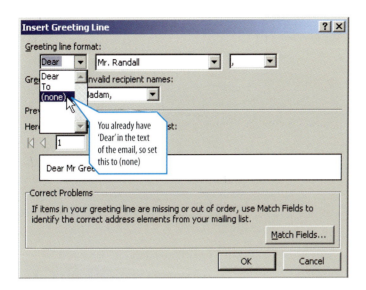

Figure 3.33

82 Click **OK**.

You should see that 'Mr Green' has been added to the space left for the salutation.

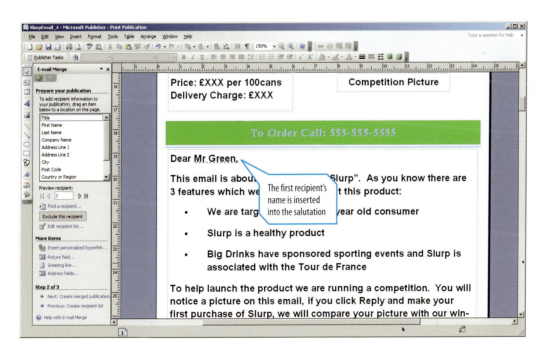

Figure 3.34

83 Now scroll down through your email text to 'Incidentally,   , it has been some time …'

We need to place a copy of the shopkeeper's first name here.

84 Place the insertion point cursor one space to the right of the first comma:

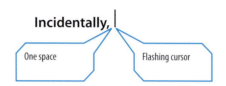

SOFTWARE SKILLS
Inserting placeholders

85 Now click **First Name** in the top panel of the E-mail Merge pane (see Figure 3.35).

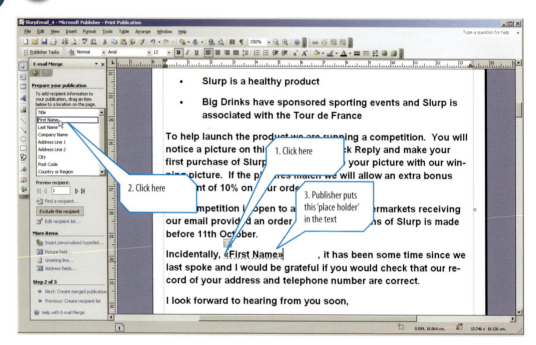

Figure 3.35

86 Notice that Publisher responds by putting

<<**First Name**>>

in the text, which acts as a 'place holder' for the various first names that will go into the text of the email at this point.

87 You will need to delete the extra spaces to the right of <<First Name>>.

88 Make an extra text box under the pale blue thin box at the bottom of the email. This is for the shopkeepers' addresses.

89 Type 'Contact Details' as a heading for the text box. Format the text to **Arial**, size **12**, **Bold**, **Black**.

90 You can use the same technique as you used for adding the First Name place holder for adding the address place holders inside the text box.

91 Click each field in turn. *Do not* bother tidying up the text box; you will get in a muddle if you do. Leave this for later once you have clicked in all of the fields, *except* the Picture Field.

Now tidy up the text box!

92 Click and press **Enter** to make a new line between:

The text box will look something like this:

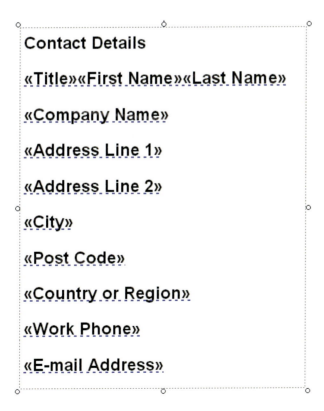

Figure 3.36

Now we need to add the Picture Field. Click in the Picture Frame above 'Competition Picture'.

 Click **Picture Field** in the E-mail Merge pane.

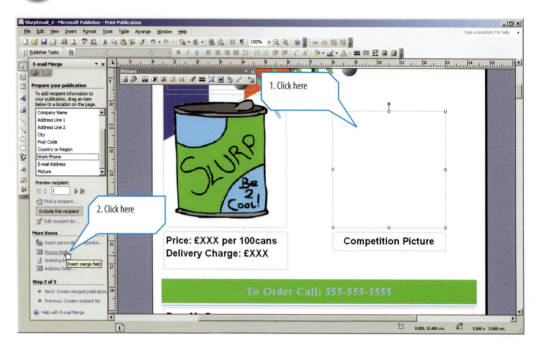

Figure 3.37

 The **Insert Picture Field** dialogue box opens.

Figure 3.38

 Scroll down and click **Picture**.

 Click **Specify Folders**.

You are now about to tell Publisher where to find the pictures that it will use to put into the emails to the shopkeepers.

98 In the **Look for pictures in these folders** pane, click on **[Data source folder]** and then click **Add**.

 99 A Browse dialogue box appears. Use this to navigate to the **SlurpEmailMerge** folder, which contains the pictures that we will need for the email to the shopkeepers.

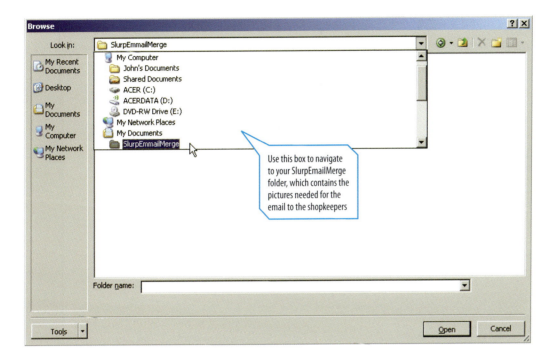

Figure 3.39

 100 Once you have found the folder, click on it and then click **Open**.

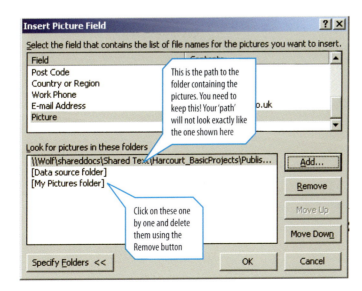

Figure 3.40

101 Click on **[Data source folder]** and click **Remove**.

 102 Click on **[My Pictures folder]** and click **Remove**.

 103 Click **OK**.

Patience! It might need a second or so, but the first image will appear.

FUNCTIONAL SKILLS

Inserting appropriate images – this shows why it is important to think about file size if using images electronically

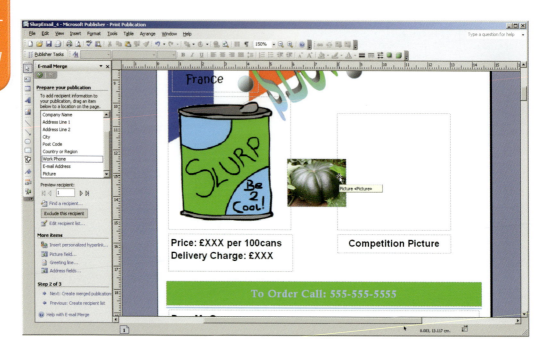

Figure 3.41

 104 Click on the image, drag it into the picture frame and resize it to fit as nearly as possible.

 105 Use the arrow buttons in the Tasks pane to check that all of the emails work correctly and have the correct data in the address, salutation, first name and pictures (see Figure 3.42).

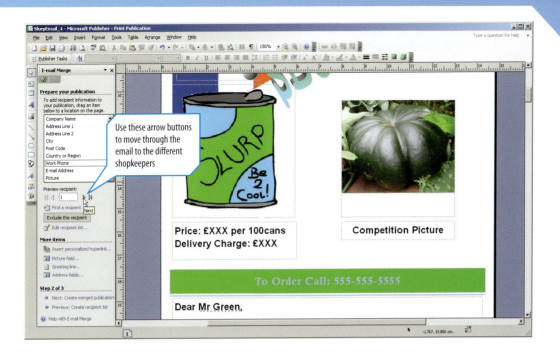

Figure 3.42

 106 Give your email a final look over to check again that everything is as it should be, then click **Next**.

Step 3

 107 The view does not change much, but if you look in the Tasks pane, you now have the option E-mail preview.

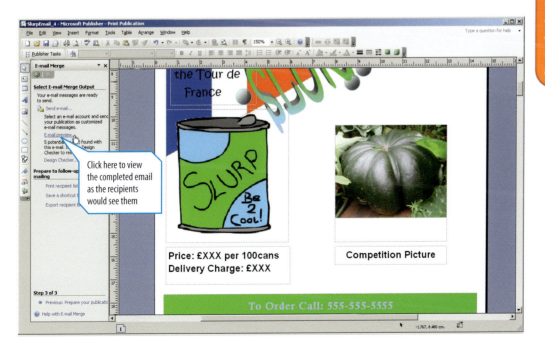

Figure 3.42

FUNCTIONAL SKILLS

Reviewing work – checking work before you send it to a customer is important so that you can catch any mistakes that you may have made or parts of the work that you have forgotten to complete – always check back with your plan. It's always a good idea to ask somebody else to read your work as you might not see the mistakes yourself

 Click **E-mail preview**.

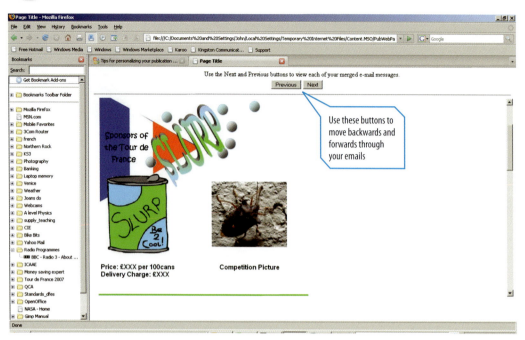

Figure 3.43

ALL DONE

That's it. There's good reason for a pat on the back!

Big Drinks go international (encore une fois)!

There are a few things that you could do to improve and extend the project.

The most obvious is that some of the formatting in the email could be improved.

Have you noticed that one of the shops is French? What about providing a translation of the Standard Letter? The controls in E-Mail Merge will allow you to select only certain recipients for the French version.

What about putting a hyperlink in the email and linking this to a 'homepage'? Big Drinks Ltd could use this homepage to inform shops about new products and forthcoming offers. The homepage needn't be a fancy website – you could experiment and get the system working just by making the email link to a page in a Word file.

CHECKPOINT

Check that you know how to:

- Select a template.

- Navigate to find a file.

- Copy and save a file in a new location.

- Use the navigation tools to find a file.

- Add assets to the Content Library.

- Re-use assets in a new project.

- Use AutoShapes.

- Format an AutoShape.

- Use graduated fill and transparency tools.

- Use keyboard shortcuts to copy and paste.

- Change the fields (column names) in a database.

- Add data to a database.

- Set place holders in a standard letter.

- Use navigation tools to set the path to link a place holder in the standard letter with pictures held in a file.

ASSESSMENT POINT

Now let's assess the work. Look back at the table at the beginning of this section (**Target point**) and decide on which of the statements you can answer 'Yes' to.

Did you do as well as you expected? Could you improve your work? Use Publisher to add a comment to your work to show what you could do to improve it and remember this when starting your next ICT project.

GET AHEAD

In the Project you will be on your own.

You will need to prepare for this, so look over the work you have done so that you are thoroughly prepared for the Project. Then you can expect to do well.

The Project

PRODUCING A POSTER AND EMAIL TICKETING SYSTEM FOR A NEW GIG

TASK BRIEF

Hades Pipistrelles is a band. They have sent you an email with the following brief:

From: Hades Pipistrelles

To: Design Studio

Project title: Gig poster and email ticketing system.

Background information: Hades Pipistrelles' next concert is to be held at Aldersley Stadium on 25 April. They will perform tracks from their latest album *Chiroptera*, as well as many of their well-known hits.

Project outline: We need a way of advertising the concert that we can place in different locations around the city and we want to try a new ticketing system. We want to try out a new way of sending out tickets so that we can cut down on the amount of paper that we use and also the costs of sending the tickets out, so we would like you to design a new email that will act as the ticket.

PROJECT REQUIREMENTS

- A poster for advertising the gig.
- An E-mail Merge ticket.

Information to be included:

- The concert will start at 7.30 and finish at 11.00.
- Tickets can only be bought online. Confirmation of allocation of a ticket is sent via email.
- Each email will be the ticket to the event and have the name and age of the person coming to the gig and a unique number to prove that they have paid.
- The band will donate 20% of the money from ticket sales to The Bat Conservation Trust.

Ticket prices are:

- £10 (over 18 years).
- £5 (under 18 years).
- £7.50 (concessions).

Level 3	Level 4	Level 5	Level 6
You have saved your work	You have saved your work in an appropriate folder	You have set up a folder structure to help you to work in a systematic manner	
You have arranged some of the files that you need	You have found and relocated the files you will need	You have shown a methodical approach: arranging files in a new folder and other needed files in the Content Library	
You can create the body of an email	You have used the E-mail Merge wizard tool to make a personalised email for several recipients	You recognise the need to check the size of the file attached	
		You have set up the database and imported all of the fields into the correct locations in the Standard Letter	You understand the advantages of the email system that makes use of a database studied in Task 3 and an example of when it would be used
	You have chosen relevant images and text for your poster and email	You have chosen the most suitable images and text for your poster and email for your audience, in your opinion	You have built into your plan how to check that you have chosen the most suitable images and text through feedback from your client
	You have used one or two keywords to search for images	You have used more than two keywords to search for images	You have used alternative methods to keywords to search for your images
			You have acknowledged the source of any information that is not your own
	You have adapted your work to use only the tools available in a single software program	You have adapted your work to use the tools available in more than one software program	You have considered the ICT software and tools that are most appropriate for your task in your plan
	You have represented your plan as a sequence of actions	You have represented your plan as a sequence of actions and built in steps to check your documents for accuracy	You have represented your plan as a sequence of actions and built in steps to check your documents for accuracy and evaluate whether it met your need

TARGET POINT

Have a look at the following statements before you start your project so you know what you are aiming for.

Level 3	Level 4	Level 5	Level 6
You have used a new template	You have used the Style controls to change an existing template including changes to show that you understand layering	You have used the Style controls to change an existing template and used it to make the style of your documents consistent	You have created your own style sheet and used it to make the style of your documents consistent
	You have combined different forms of information into your document and styled it appropriately for your audience		
		You have made your document suitable for an unfamiliar audience	
			You have compared your work with other similar documents and listened to feedback and revised your work as necessary
	You have used the criteria and met most of the requirements of the brief	You have used the criteria and met all of the requirements of the brief and produced a template appropriate for the target audience	

To meet this project brief you need to complete the poster and the ticket that can be emailed, but that is only one part of the process that you would need to go through if you were designing these for a real band. The information below shows you how you could go about planning your documents, but you need to show what you would do to review the information. Use the target points to decide how and which of the other steps you want to tackle.

The Functional Skills listed below show you the skills you will be demonstrating in your work – but remember you have to know *why* you have chosen to demonstrate them in a particular way and how your choices match your audience and purpose for the documents.

> Planning your documents.

> Using suitable software for your poster and ticket.

> Saving your documents with suitable filenames.

> Using a suitable template and document layout.

> Editing text with suitable fonts, colours and styles.

> Inserting and editing images.

> Sending an email.

> Testing and reviewing your documents.

ADVICE

There are two tasks – the poster and the E-mail Merge. But before you start, you should do some planning. Complete these sections and think of any more columns that you should add – what about styles and reviewing by you and the customer?

Poster

What is the purpose of the poster?	Target audience	What information needs to be displayed in the poster?	What might be suitable images?	Where might I research suitable images?	How will I edit the images?
	Age range				
	Likes/dislikes				

E-Mail Merge

You might want to include some of the columns from your planning for the poster too.

How does the ticket sales system work?	What items must be in the email?		Which fields need to be included in the email?	
	1		1	
↓	2		2	
↓	3		3	
↓	4		4	
↓	5		5	

SOFTWARE

Type of software	Advantage	Disadvantage
DTP		
Word processor		

 I am going to use DTP because ....

 The DTP application that I am going to use is called ....

Now it's your turn!

INDEX